ALSO BY BARBARA SMITH

B. Smith's Entertaining and Cooking for Friends

To David Ross & Family

Enjoy, ease my book

with style

B. Smith

B. SMITH

RITUALS & CELEBRATIONS

B. SMITH
RITUALS&CELEBRATIONS

Barbara Smith

Photographs by Mark Ferri

RANDOM HOUSE NEW YORK

Copyright © 1999 by Barbara Smith
Photographs copyright © 1999 by Mark Ferri

RANDOM HOUSE and colophon are registered trademarks of Random House, Inc.

Designed by Joel Avirom and Jason Snyder
Design Assistant: Meghan Day Healey

Library of Congress Cataloging-in-Publication Data
Smith, Barbara.
    B. Smith: rituals & celebrations / by Barbara Smith.
      p.   cm.
    Includes index.
    ISBN 0-375-50236-X
    1. Holiday cookery. 2. Entertaining. I. Title.
  TX739.S485   1999
  641.5'68—dc21   99-24504

Random House website address: www.atrandom.com

98765432
First Edition

For the Great Gasby,
my lover, my husband, my friend

———

CONTENTS

INTRODUCTION

I get a huge amount of satisfaction out of creating lasting memories. That's one reason I've made celebrations such a major part of my life. When you really throw yourself into preparing something that you're sharing with other people, something that comes from your heart—whether it's your own version of a Chinese New Year dinner or a keepsake Valentine's collage— you create a memory that lasts forever. And, of course, every time you celebrate one of the traditional holidays, you become part of a whole chain of memories woven by the generations that came before you and those that are following after.

The other reason that celebrations are so important to me is simple: I love to have fun. Celebrating something, anything, gives me an excuse. It's more than the fun of everyone having a good time; it's the fun of feeling inspired to try something new, and going with it: an unexpected color, a surprising twist on an old recipe, or a whole new reason to celebrate whatever wakes you up and makes you feel! As you leaf through each month of celebrations I've described in this book, you'll find new and unusual rituals for ancient celebrations, along with a year's worth of new excuses to create such memorable occasions as a Labor Day dinner party on the beach, a Juneteenth feast, a bid whist party, or an at-home wine-tasting—there's no limit to the possibilities. One friend of mine had a Bark Mitzvah for her two dogs. And why not?

This book combines both my passions: carrying on traditions that keep our pasts alive and creating new ones that celebrate who we are now. It's not so much about Christmases and birthdays as it is about the birth of ideas, ideas for celebrations and rituals whose memories can live with you and take you through the down times. I think that we all as human beings want to be touched by experiences. You can be having one of the worst days of your life, and suddenly an unforgettable fragrance, even a taste or a color, can take you back to a special event and the people with whom you shared it.

I think that part of the reason we all love the traditional celebrations is because they give us the chance to indulge in rituals that still taste of the excitement we felt in our childhood, like when we decorated the Christmas tree or smelled fall in the air on Thanksgiving. Any ritual has the power to transport us beyond the day-to-day, even the ones we create for ourselves. When you soak in a bathtub with your favorite soap every night, it might seem mundane, but you have actually created a ritual; it's your way of removing the stresses of daily living. Rituals that go along with celebrations also help us mark the beginnings and endings that give shape to our lives: a new year, a coming of age, the first day of spring.

You'll find a calendar year of traditional celebrations in these pages. Some of them have evolved from traditions I grew up with or ones my husband, Dan, brought to our relationship from his childhood. I've adapted them to fit our lives. Unlike the families we came from, ours is a small one: myself, Dan, and my thirteen-year-old stepdaughter, Dana. Some of the celebrations have been shaped by my experiences traveling around the world as a model, experiencing different cultures. I've always enjoyed sharing these experiences with others. Traveling, and growing up in a town that was home to people from a whole variety of ethnic backgrounds, taught me that there's no right or wrong way to go about celebrating even the most traditional of holidays.

Some of the other celebrations you'll find here are my inventions. It's up to you to take what you like of these ideas and add whatever suits your sense of fun or satisfies your personal sense of tradition. Borrow, change, invent—just as I've taken what was passed down to me and given it a new twist that expresses my world and my personality. It's one of the great things about reaching adulthood: As a child, you have to do things the way your family does them; as a grown-up, you can create and re-create all you want.

Some of the best ideas come from the most unexpected places; mine can come from movies, a store window display I happen to see, or an old novel I'm reading. That's why in this book I encourage you to trust in your moments of inspiration and follow your impulses. Invent new rituals; in time, they'll become part of the family. Create new traditions: Instead of a single tree for Christmas, why not have two or three, all decorated with a different thought in mind? For Valentine's Day, skip the red roses for a change and get the dinner table (and yourself) all decked out in hot pink.

You don't need vast resources to be creative. You just have to be resourceful. Most of the recipes you'll find in this book give a new twist to basic everyday ingredients, and the craft projects make use of materials you're likely to have lying around the house. Beauty can come from the simplest beginnings. That's what I learned from my mother who was an extraordinary hostess and a craftsperson long before it gained the popularity it has today.

Food traditions, an important element of any celebration, are open to all kinds of innovation. There's no way you can have a birthday party without a cake or Thanksgiving dinner without a turkey. But a birthday cake doesn't have to be covered with buttercream frosting and roses. Some people I know prefer to arrange birthday candles as a unique centerpiece for the table, and serve fruit instead of the traditional birthday cake.

I hope this book inspires you to create events that add something special to your life year after year, just as my nontraditional celebration of mothers and others on Mother's Day is now an annual event, as is Spring Hooky Day, a once-a-year ritual in which friends and I escape from the usual routine and slip away for a day of relaxing kicked off with a wonderful luncheon. Take your inspiration from anything that is unique and special about you and your family and friends. If you are a great gardener, give an outdoor party when your plants are in their fullest bloom. If your kitchen is attractive, plan a party where guests are invited to help themselves to the food directly off the stove. If someone plays an instrument, hold a recital or a sing-along or a Christmas carol party so he or she can perform. If someone likes to heat up the dance floor or dress up, plan a dance or throw a costume party.

Find ways to add your own creative touch to every menu and recipe, every table decoration, and every event. Play with ideas, break the rules, have some fun. Make it a family tradition to turn convention on its head by starting a birthday celebration with cake and ice cream for breakfast. Have green eggs on St. Patrick's Day. You and the people in your world can share so much pleasure by creating rituals that are uniquely yours, and then making them part of a celebration that's repeated year after year.

NOTE: In order to spend less time in the kitchen and more time celebrating with friends and family, I'll occasionally use a store-bought item on a menu. I've indicated these menu items in smaller type. Of course, you may want to prepare a homemade version of a store-bought item since it's all about making these rituals and celebrations your own.

B. SMITH
RITUALS & CELEBRATIONS

JANUARY

A NEW YEAR'S DAY BUFFET

I love the idea of being able to start anew. For me, that's the great thing about New Year's Day. I'm not talking so much about resolutions—those "shoulds" and "musts" for the future—as about setting the spirit for the year ahead through the way we celebrate, whom we celebrate with, and the kinds of rituals we borrow or invent.

I've celebrated New Year's Day in many different ways. Years ago, one of the big things for me and my friends was to have an outdoor barbecue party, no matter what the weather. You never knew if it was going to be sunny or snowing—and that was half the fun. But all that was in another life. Though these parties were terrific, they took a little more work and offered a lot less comfort than I want now. Besides, these days I like a more elegant start to my year.

In *this* life, my husband, Dan, and I have enjoyed going to our favorite spa for a luxurious start to the months ahead; and for several years, we made it a tradition to attend a friend's annual New Year's Day open house and potluck dinner. But nowadays what I

As I put the finishing touches on the table,
I use candles to help create a cozy atmosphere.

enjoy most is to gather close friends together for my own relaxed, late-afternoon New Year's Day buffet. My experience as a hostess has been that when people come into your home and share your rituals, they learn a little bit more about who you are, no matter how well they know you.

People in many different cultures have some type of New Year's Day ritual, and most of these rituals involve superstition. Dan's mother had a lovely New Year ritual that came from a superstition concerning the first person to enter your home. Every year "Miss Louise," as she was called, would select a good-natured, warm-spirited person to come to the house—it could be anyone from a toddler to an elder. Then she would walk the chosen one through each room in the house, hoping the person would bring luck, peace, harmony, and good health to her family. In exchange for these services, she offered a crisp, new ten-dollar bill.

I'm not exactly sure how my mother-in-law came by this custom, but I've learned of similar New Year superstitions in other cultures. A traditional Scottish belief, for example, is that the first person in your door will set the tone for the next year. And the Portuguese say that the way you conduct yourself on January 1 will serve as a pattern for the next twelve months.

You don't have to be superstitious to get a kick out of borrowing rituals like these, especially if they're a part of your own family or cultural tradition. At my New Year's Day party, I serve foods that were part of my childhood, and that in my family's tradition represented everything you could possibly wish for in your future: For example, greens, being the color of money, symbolized wealth; fish was considered brain food; black-eyed peas in the hoppin' John, a classic Southern New Year's Day dish, were supposed to bring luck; put a dime into the dish with the peas and you might even guarantee yourself an influx of money all year! I like to incorporate in our family life certain things my parents or Dan's did—whether we're doing it for the same reason they did or in honor of the reason they did it. And though I don't think of myself as a superstitious person, I can't help thinking that if it worked for them, why not give it a try?

Some of the foods I use in my New Year's Day menu are not so much symbolic as familiar—ingredients that my mother used to cook with, and that take me and many of my guests back to the jaw breakers and first pets of our child-

hoods. After all the formality of New Year's Eve, with its sequins and Champagne, these comfort foods help everyone feel at home and relaxed.

But while my mother used these ingredients to prepare exactly the same dishes year after year, I've come up with some interesting variations tailored to my guests' tastes. My mother might have made fried catfish instead of snapper, and chitlins instead of my special pork tenderloin. She always made sweet potato pie and candied yams; instead, I make sweet potato stuffing for the pork and use the candied glaze to coat it. For me, that's the fun of cooking: taking the old and making it new.

Since Dan and I celebrate into the wee hours on New Year's Eve at our restaurant in New York and sleep in the next morning, I prepare whatever I can of the meal the day before: I clean the winter greens, bag them, and make the vinaigrette; mix spices for the snapper; and cook the Southern-style greens, which can be refrigerated overnight. The hoppin' John can be made in advance, too. Then, come New Year's Day, all I have to do is finish off the preparations and get ready for late-afternoon visitors. The great thing about this time of year is that the house is already decorated, so I can focus on the food and the table setting—something elegant but casual and toned-down. This year, it's sparkling silver serving platters, plum, green, and silver candles, and some sprigs of holiday greens.

This isn't a big day for sweets. The meal is so hearty and satisfying, filled with such a complex mix of sweet and savory flavors, that there are rarely many takers for dessert. But I do offer the adults a choice of coffee and liqueurs, and I always stock the bar with a variety of wines to suit everyone's taste. Because people tend to want to bring something on New Year's Day, I might suggest some special breads, a dessert liqueur, or a favorite blend of coffee.

This is an occasion for very relaxed entertaining, and Dan and I encourage our guests to make themselves comfortable in whatever ways they please. He's part of a group of guys ensconced in front of the TV watching the football games. A couple of folks will curl up in a cozy corner and listen to music, and others prefer to chat. That still leaves a few who want to spend the whole time in the kitchen. As for the kids, no sooner have they greeted one another at the door than they're disappearing into Dana's room, not to be seen again until it's time to eat. Then everyone takes a plate and settles in on the sofa near the coffee table or sinks into a favorite cushy chair.

Since the first day of the year is also the last day of Kwanzaa, at some point during the afternoon we'll all go sit around the kanara and reiterate the seven principles of Kwanzaa. It's always interesting to those guests who are not African American that these principles—which include unity, creativity, and purpose—are so universal. It brings people together.

When you have in your house elements of how you celebrate, guests tend to get that warm, comfortable feeling and leave your home on a high note. To help that high note along, I like to give everybody a little package to go home with. Many cultures exchange some type of gift for the New Year. These may be simply gifts from the heart. In some European countries, it's a custom for schoolchildren to write letters to members of their immediate family, sending them good wishes and laying out their resolutions for the New Year. In France, family and friends give one another chocolates, preserved fruit, and candied chestnuts.

In giving small gifts, my theme has always been that it doesn't matter how expensive they are; people enjoy the thoughtfulness and originality behind them. One year, when we visited friends for New Year's Day, I brought for each couple a little bag with two miniature bottles of liqueur to fit their personalities—a split of Champagne with a pair of tiny glasses for a really bubbly couple; Jägermeister for a pair of eternal college sweethearts. These days, my gift of choice is both a token of my heartfelt wishes for my closest friends and a joke on the fact that on New Year's Day, everybody is thinking about whether they're going to have health, wealth, and happiness in the coming year.

This is a day for people to gather into a cozy corner and enjoy one another's company.

HEALTH, WEALTH, AND WISDOM PACKAGE

A New Year's favor to send home with your guests

MATERIALS

One per guest:

    packet of vitamins

    lottery ticket

    small book

several yards of sheer fabric

ribbon

scissors

tissue paper

1 Pick up one pack of vitamins per guest from your local drug- or health store, where they often have small assortments at the checkout counter; a lottery ticket; and, for each guest, also purchase a miniature book of poetry, wisdom, or quotes at the bookstore.

2 Bundle the gifts in a pretty fabric, such as organza, edged with pinking shears. You can use one or more colors and finish off the package with a contrasting ribbon tie. I used an elegant, deep purple tassle.

3 If you prefer, add a little colored tissue paper to the bottom of a Chinese food container and place the items inside. Instead of takeout containers, you can use easy-to-find, inexpensive mesh bags (people can use them later for their jewelry when they travel).

4 Group the packages together on a tray or in a basket, or stack them on a cake plate. They'll add a decorative touch—and probably some laughs— to the party.

A New Year's Day
Buffet for Eight

Winter Salad with
Blood Orange Vinaigrette

—

Roasted Spiced Whole Red Snapper

Candied Glazed Pork Tenderloin
with Sweet Potato Stuffing

—

Southern-Style Greens

—

Hoppin' John

Coffee and liqueurs

—

Domaine Chandon Reserve (or any other sparkling wine)

Chardonnay, Stonestreet, Sonoma County, 1995
(or any other Chardonnay)

Pinot Noir, Talus, California, 1996 (or any other Pinot Noir)

Pineau des Charentes (or any other dessert wine)

*Clockwise from top right: Winter Salad with Blood Orange
Vinaigrette, Candied Glazed Pork Tenderloin with Sweet
Potato Stuffing, Southern-Style Greens, Roasted Spiced
Whole Red Snapper, Hoppin' John*

WINTER SALAD with BLOOD ORANGE VINAIGRETTE

This tangy, sweet-and-sour dressing makes the salad a good contrast to the heavier side dishes. Blood oranges, which are in season at this time of the year, add zip. But if you can't find blood oranges, regular fresh-squeezed orange juice and pulp will do just fine. **SERVES 8**

¼ cup fresh-squeezed blood orange juice or orange juice

2 tablespoons lemon juice

1½ teaspoons Dijon mustard

¼ teaspoon salt

⅛ teaspoon sugar

Freshly ground black pepper to taste

⅔ cup extra virgin olive oil

10 cups mixed watercress, radicchio, and endive leaves

In a small bowl, whisk together the orange juice, the lemon juice, mustard, salt, sugar, and pepper. Whisk in the olive oil until well blended. Pour the dressing over the salad and serve immediately.

ROASTED SPICED WHOLE RED SNAPPER

The skin of the whole snapper is a true red, and the fish itself is lean yet succulent. It's wonderful either baked, as it is here, or simply grilled with a squeeze of lemon. When making the sauce, if you use Pineau des Charentes, which I prefer—a combination of cognac and young wine—you will have a slightly sweet sauce. If you use dry white wine, the sauce will be more savory. **SERVES 8**

Two 3-pound whole red snappers, cleaned

Juice of 2 lemons

2 tablespoons Old Bay Seasoning

2 tablespoons paprika

¼ cup extra virgin olive oil

1 cup Pineau des Charentes or dry white wine

2 bunches watercress, washed and dried

Cut three or four crosswise slashes into both sides of each fish. Sprinkle lemon juice on both sides and inside the cavity of the fish. Combine the Old Bay Seasoning and paprika; sprinkle inside and outside of each fish. Wrap fish tightly in plastic wrap and marinate, refrigerated, for at least 1 hour.

Preheat the oven to 450 degrees. In a large, oiled roasting pan, arrange the fish and drizzle with the olive oil. Place in the oven and bake 25 to 35 minutes, until the flesh is opaque. Remove the fish to a serving platter and keep warm while preparing the sauce. Place the roasting pan on top of the stove over medium heat. Add the Pineau des Charentes and bring to a boil. Reduce the heat and simmer 2 to 3 minutes, until slightly reduced and syrupy. Strain the sauce and pour over the fish.

Arrange the watercress around the fish and serve immediately.

CANDIED GLAZED PORK TENDERLOIN
WITH SWEET POTATO STUFFING

In this recipe, I combine some of my favorite foods—pork tenderloin (a choice cut), sweet potatoes, and raisin bread—in one easy-to-prepare dish.   SERVES 8

3 tablespoons butter

2 cups diced sweet potato

½ cup diced onion

½ cup diced celery

1½ cups cubed dried cinnamon-raisin bread (½-inch cubes)

1¼ teaspoons ground cinnamon, divided

Salt and freshly ground black pepper to taste

2 or 3 pork tenderloins, butterflied (about 3 pounds total weight)

3 tablespoons orange marmalade

2 tablespoons orange juice

2 tablespoons brown sugar

⅛ teaspoon ground ginger

3 tablespoons olive oil

In a skillet over medium heat, melt the butter. Add the sweet potato, onion, and celery, and sauté until the sweet potato is tender, about 6 minutes. Stir in the cubed bread and ¼ teaspoon of the cinnamon; season with salt and pepper. Set aside to cool.

Slightly flatten each tenderloin; season both sides with salt and pepper. Evenly divide the sweet potato stuffing mixture between the tenderloins. Reshape the tenderloins to enclose the stuffing; tie with kitchen twine or secure with skewers.

Preheat the oven to 400 degrees. In a small bowl, stir together the marmalade, orange juice, brown sugar, ginger, and remaining 1 teaspoon of cinnamon.

In a large ovenproof skillet or sauté pan over medium-high heat, heat the olive oil. Sear the tenderloins on all sides. Transfer the skillet to the oven and roast 5 minutes. Brush the tenderloins with some of the marmalade mixture and return to the oven for 5 minutes. Brush again with glaze and continue roasting 5 to 10 minutes, until the outsides are a rich brown and the tenderloins are firm to the touch.

Let the tenderloins stand 10 minutes before removing twine or skewers and cutting into ½-inch slices to serve.

SOUTHERN-STYLE GREENS

SERVES 8

4 smoked ham hocks
1 large onion, thinly sliced
3 bay leaves
4 pounds collard, kale, and mustard greens, well cleaned
Chicken stock or water
2 teaspoons crushed red pepper
1 teaspoon salt
1 teaspoon freshly ground black pepper

Rinse the ham hocks and score the skin in several places. In a heavy 8- to 10-quart pot, combine the hocks, onion, and bay leaves with enough water to cover. Bring to a boil, reduce heat, and simmer, covered, 1½ to 2 hours, until the hocks are falling apart. Remove from the heat. Remove the ham hocks and reserve the meat, discarding the bones, skin, and fat. Strain the cooking liquid, degrease it, and return it to the pot.

While the ham hocks are cooking, remove the stems from the greens and roughly chop; set aside.

Add enough chicken stock or water to the ham stock to make 6 cups. Add the chopped greens, red pepper, salt, black pepper, and reserved ham. Bring to a simmer and cook 45 minutes to 1 hour.

Candied Glazed Pork Tenderloin
with Sweet Potato Stuffing

HOPPIN' JOHN

I love the flavor salt pork adds to this traditional New Year's Day dish. If you prefer, diced smoked turkey would be a good substitute for salt pork.   SERVES 8

2 cups dried black-eyed peas
4 cups chicken broth
4 ounces diced salt pork
1 large onion, chopped
1 cup chopped green bell pepper
2 cloves garlic, minced
2 bay leaves
½ teaspoon dried thyme leaves
½ teaspoon freshly ground black pepper
¼ teaspoon ground cayenne pepper
1½ cups uncooked rice
¼ cup chopped fresh parsley

In a large bowl, place the black-eyed peas and cover with cold water. Let soak overnight. Drain the peas; rinse thoroughly.

In a large saucepan or Dutch oven, combine the peas with the remaining ingredients except the rice and parsley. Bring to a boil over high heat. Reduce the heat to low, cover, and simmer 45 to 60 minutes, until peas are firm but tender. Add the rice; cover and continue cooking 20 to 25 minutes, until the rice is done.

Sprinkle with the chopped parsley before serving.

A Chinese New Year Dinner

When I first moved to New York as a young woman and had boundless energy to dance the night away, my friends and I would often end a very late evening—or, I should say, welcome a very early morning—with a meal in Chinatown. The tourist places would have long since closed, but the kitchens were still busy at the authentic restaurants on Mott Street, where the menus were written only in Chinese.

It was very hip back then to go down to Chinatown, but I think I would have gravitated there anyway. Many things lured me besides the restaurants. I bought clingy, shiny *cheong-sams,* those truly elegant Chinese dresses with the two-button closing at the collarbone. I spent hours wandering around the shops piled high with plates, bowls, and cups painted with a seemingly endless variety of delicate and colorful designs, imagining the pretty tabletops I could create if I owned them all. I stopped at stand after stand to examine the heaping displays of exotic fruits and vegetables and intriguing varieties of fish, some dried and some so fresh they were still swimming in pails. I wandered into herbalist shops to poke through shelves full of teas and roots and different varieties of packaged ginseng.

Things Chinese fascinated me long before I made an early trip to Beijing. I love the culture, I'm fascinated by the aesthetic and all of its attention to detail, and I especially adore the food. So after several years of participating in my chef Henry's annual Chinese New Year banquet at B. Smith's in New York, I decided to try my own version at home with my family and friends. I always like to create celebrations from different cultures in my own environment. It's fun, it's interesting, and it's quite a challenge. Pretty soon, Chinese New Year at our house became a family tradition—with a slightly un-Chinese twist.

The New Year in China is based on a lunar calendar and can fall on any date between January 21 and February 19. (It falls on February 5 in the year 2000, and on January 24 in 2001.) We celebrate on the holiday eve. Never one to miss an opportunity to play dress-up, I get into the spirit of the occasion by decking myself out in a turquoise robe I brought back from China, or, some years, in one of my *cheong-sams.* I've even thought about slipping into a pair of silky Chinese pajamas.

I've always loved the color red, and when Chinese New Year comes around, I get to go overboard with it because in

Always one to dress the part, for this dinner party I chose to wear a Chinese kimono that I brought back from a trip to Beijing.

China, red is the color of good fortune. When I design my table setting, I start with a red cloth, red votives, and some red silk napkins I made with a piece of fabric from Chinatown, patterned with the Chinese character for "eternal happiness." Any solid-patterned silk would do, though. I'm sure that in China there's a whole palette of symbolic colors for New Year, but my take on the celebration is playful rather than correct, so after red, I add a jewel green—the color of Chinese jade, and I top it off with a deep blue—the blue you see in so many Chinese ceramics.

When I was in Beijing, I bought a few dolls representing characters from the Chinese opera. Liberated from my closet, they make a colorful centerpiece. But the highlight of my Chinese New Year table, a little gift for each guest, is something you can find in any pet store: goldfish swimming in goldfish bowls.

According to the Chinese system of feng shui, little details in the way you decorate your home (reflections in a mirror positioned in just the right spot, the sound of potted bamboo rustling near a window) can have a positive influence on your mental and physical well-being. I thought the small flashes of gold movement in water at each place setting would be energizing—or, at least, surprising!

Goldfish might even bring good fortune. Like the color red, orange is considered lucky in China, and orange fruits are traditionally served on New Year's Day; the Chinese word for "tangerine" is similar to the word for "luck." If you want to go along with the holiday food symbolism, serve round foods like dumplings for togetherness, green foods for growth, or a whole fish for family unity.

Though these dishes include egg drop soup, fried rice, dumplings, roast duck, and spring rolls, this meal isn't strictly authentic. (You're not likely to find apple-stuffed spring rolls with rum-cider syrup—my New Year dessert—on any Chinese banquet table!) The truth is, it's virtually impossible to create a really authentic dish unless you're a serious student of the cuisine. So you have to improvise. Nobody can do roast duck better than the Chinese, but I thought it would be fun to mix heritages and have duck with spiced pineapple. My recipe for dumplings is based on one given to me by Philadelphia restaurateur Susanna Foo, except instead of her pork filling, I used shrimp. If you can't find baby corn and snow peas for the fried rice, substitute carrots and corn kernels. The idea is to take flavors that you and your guests are familiar with and make your own version of the traditional menu in celebration of the culture. Mixing and matching flavors makes cooking—and eating—exciting.

Though I like to drink endless cups of green tea with Chinese food, most of my guests prefer to have wine with the meal. So I make a pot of tea available for anyone who shares my passion, and serve the tea with the apple spring rolls.

Before people leave with their goldfish, we open fortune cookies, which I buy at my favorite Chinese restaurant. It's an essential ritual on Chinese New Year, even though after consuming so much delicious food at such a lucky-colored table, my guests already feel not only very well fed, but also very positive about the prospects for the coming year!

A Chinese New Year Dinner for Six

Shrimp Dumplings
with Ginger Soy Sauce

Egg Drop Soup

Roast Duck with
Spiced Pineapple

Sautéed Baby Bok Choy

Vegetable Fried Rice

Warm Apple Spring Rolls
with Rum-Cider Syrup

Fortune cookies

Green tea

Fumé Blanc, Dry Creek, Sonoma County, 1994
(or any other fumé blanc)

SHRIMP DUMPLINGS WITH GINGER SOY SAUCE

SERVES 6

½ pound fresh or frozen raw shrimp,
shelled, deveined, and minced,
(about 1¼ cups)

2 scallions, chopped very fine (about
3 to 4 tablespoons)

1 tablespoon chopped fresh ginger

1 cup finely chopped green cabbage

1 tablespoon sesame oil

1 tablespoon hoisin sauce or soy sauce

½ teaspoon salt

¼ teaspoon freshly ground pepper

One 12-ounce package round egg roll
or wonton wrappers, 3 to 4 inches
in diameter, fresh or thawed frozen
(available in most grocery stores)

1 tablespoon olive oil

¼ cup water

Ginger Soy Sauce (recipe follows)

In a medium bowl, toss the minced shrimp and all other ingredients except the wrappers, olive oil, and water. Allow to marinate at least 30 minutes and up to 2 hours, covered and refrigerated.

Line a tray or baking sheet with waxed paper. Set aside. Place one egg roll or wonton wrapper on a clean, dry work surface. Keep the remaining wrappers in plastic wrap. Mound 1 level tablespoon of filling in the center. Have a small dish of water handy near the work surface. Lightly moisten the edge of the wrapper with a finger dipped in cold water and fold wrapper in half to form a half-moon, pressing down around the filling to force out air and sealing the edges well. Moisten the pointed ends of the dumpling and bring them together, carefully curling the dumpling around the tip of your index finger to form a ring. Press the ends gently together, overlapping to form a seal. Transfer the dumpling to the tray, standing it on the flat side. Repeat until you have made a total of 18 dumplings. (You will have enough wrappers and enough filling left over to make approximately eight more dumplings, which you can freeze.)

The dumplings may be made 2 hours ahead and refrigerated, covered with a damp paper towel. Or they may be made 1 month ahead and frozen. (To freeze: Put the dumplings in the freezer on a tray loosely covered with plastic wrap until firm, about an hour, then transfer to a heavy-duty sealable plastic bag. Seal the bag, pressing out excess air. Do not thaw the dumplings before cooking.)

Brush a 12-inch nonstick skillet with the olive oil and heat over moderately high heat until hot but not smoking. Arrange the dumplings in the skillet so they aren't touching, flat sides down. Immediately pour ¼ cup water quickly around the edge of the skillet. Cover and cook the dumplings over low to medium heat until the water is evaporated and the bottoms are golden brown and slightly crisp, about 8 to 10 minutes. Or cook dumplings on their sides, checking after 4 minutes and turning to the side so both sides are golden and crisp. Serve immediately with ginger soy sauce.

GINGER SOY SAUCE

¾ cup soy sauce
1 tablespoon minced fresh ginger
1 tablespoon chopped scallion

Stir the soy sauce and ginger together. Pour into a small dipping bowl. Garnish with scallions sprinkled on top.

EGG DROP SOUP

Although soothing egg drop soup is familiar to just about everyone who has ever tasted Chinese cuisine, most people have probably never tried to make it at home. But it's quite easy to prepare. Everyone likes it; it's a good dish to serve on a cold winter's night and a perfect starter course for this special menu.   SERVES 6

6 cups chicken stock
(homemade if possible)
2 tablespoons soy sauce
1½ tablespoons cornstarch
3 tablespoons water
3 tablespoons dry sherry
2 teaspoons vegetable oil
2 large eggs
Salt and freshly ground pepper to taste
3 tablespoons chopped scallions

In a large saucepan, bring the stock to a boil, add the soy sauce, and reduce the heat to simmer. In a small bowl, stir the cornstarch and water together until smooth. Pour the mixture slowly into the stock, whisking constantly until it is incorporated. Simmer, stirring occasionally, until the broth is slightly thickened. Add the sherry, stirring gently. You may keep this mixture simmering on very low heat until you are ready to complete and serve.

Five minutes before serving, turn the heat up to medium. Whisk together the oil, eggs, salt, and pepper. Pour the egg mixture slowly, in a large circle, into the simmering stock, stirring gently. Do not overmix. Adjust the seasoning. Ladle into warm bowls. Garnish with chopped scallions.

ROAST DUCK WITH SPICED PINEAPPLE

SERVES 6

Three 5- to 6-pound ducks, cut in half
¼ cup soy sauce
½ cup hoisin sauce
¼ cup honey
½ cup rice-wine vinegar
½ cup vegetable or peanut oil
2 tablespoons grated fresh ginger
2 cloves garlic, chopped
1 tablespoon red pepper flakes
Spiced Pineapple (recipe follows)

Rinse the ducks in cold water. Pat dry with paper towels. If time allows, refrigerate the ducks lightly covered for 24 hours to help dry out the skin and make it crispier. In a large bowl, combine all the other ingredients and whisk until mixed.

Place the ducks in large, heavy-duty sealable plastic bags. Pour the marinade over the ducks in equal amounts. Squeeze out air and seal the bags. Refrigerate 6 to 8 hours, turning occasionally.

Preheat oven to 525 degrees. Arrange the ducks, skin side up, on a rack in a large roasting pan. With a sharp fork or paring knife, prick the skin all over on each duck to allow moisture to escape. Place a sheet of aluminum foil lightly over the ducks. Roast for 20 minutes. Reduce the temperature to 350 degrees. Continue roasting, basting occasionally, for 15 minutes per pound, about 1¼ to 1½ hours. Remove the foil for the last 5 minutes of roasting. The skin should be crispy and deep golden brown.

Remove the ducks from the oven. Transfer to a warm serving platter and serve immediately, with Spiced Pineapple mounded on each plate next to the duck. Or, if you prefer, you can allow the ducks to cool for up to ½ hour, then return them to the oven at 500 degrees for 5 minutes to crisp up the skin. (To check for doneness, you can use a meat thermometer. The temperature should read 190 degrees.)

NOTE: During roasting, you may want to drain excess fat from the roasting pan using a baster.

SPICED PINEAPPLE

YIELDS ABOUT 3 CUPS

3 cups fresh pineapple, cut into ¼-inch cubes
2 teaspoons grated fresh ginger
1 tablespoon honey
1 teaspoon soy sauce
¼ cup finely chopped scallions

Combine all ingredients in a small bowl. Toss until mixed. Cover and chill.

SAUTÉED BABY BOK CHOY

Bok choy is a member of the cabbage family, but feel free to substitute cabbage or large bok choy if the small one is unavailable. You may use fewer heads, but you still need the equivalent of 6 cups.   SERVES 6

2 tablespoons butter

½ medium onion, diced

⅓ cup chicken stock

½ teaspoon salt

¼ teaspoon freshly ground black pepper

6 heads baby bok choy, washed and chopped roughly (about 6 cups)

In a large skillet, melt the butter. Add the onion and sauté over medium heat until softened. Add the chicken stock, salt, and pepper; cook 3 minutes or until the stock is heated. Add bok choy and sauté, tossing, 3 to 4 minutes until wilted and tender. Serve immediately.

VEGETABLE FRIED RICE

SERVES 6

6 tablespoons vegetable oil

6 cups cooked long-grain rice

1½ cups chopped scallions

4 large eggs

1 cup each cooked vegetables (corn or baby cobs, peas or snow peas, diced carrots)

Salt and freshly ground black pepper to taste

3 tablespoons soy sauce

½ cup chopped fresh parsley

In a 12- to 14-inch nonstick skillet, heat 2 tablespoons of the oil over moderately high heat until hot but not smoking. Add the rice, tossing and stirring until hot and slightly crisp. Transfer the rice to a bowl and set aside. Heat 2 more tablespoons of the oil in the skillet. Add the scallions, cooking until softened. While the scallions are cooking, lightly beat the eggs and add to the scallions. Cook, scrambling and breaking the mixture into small pieces until lightly browned. Transfer the eggs and scallions to the bowl with the rice. Heat the remaining oil in the skillet. Add the vegetables, tossing until heated. Add soy sauce. Immediately return the rice, eggs, and scallions to the skillet. Cook, tossing, until all ingredients are heated through. Add salt and pepper to taste. Spoon onto a large, warm serving platter. Garnish with the parsley. Serve with extra soy sauce.

WARM APPLE SPRING ROLLS WITH RUM-CIDER SYRUP

SERVES 6

2 tablespoons butter

4 large Macintosh or Granny Smith apples, peeled and thinly sliced, about ¼-inch thick

½ cup brown sugar

¼ cup granulated sugar

1 teaspoon ground cinnamon

¼ teaspoon ground nutmeg

¼ teaspoon salt

12 egg roll wrappers, at least 4 inches in diameter, fresh or thawed frozen

1 egg yolk, beaten slightly

1 cup vegetable oil

Rum-Cider Syrup (recipe follows)

Powdered sugar

In a skillet on medium heat, melt the butter. Add the apples, brown and granulated sugars, the cinnamon, nutmeg, and salt. Sauté until tender, but not mushy. The apples should appear glazed after about 10 to 12 minutes. Set aside.

To make the spring rolls, line a tray with waxed paper. Make sure the wrappers measure 4 inches across. If they are larger, use kitchen shears to cut the circles down to make 4-inch circles. Place a wrapper on a clean, dry work surface. Place ¼ cup sautéed apples on the bottom half of the wrapper. Lift the edge closest to you up and over the apples and tuck the edge under apples. Roll away from you one time. Fold the left and right edges in, then continue to roll. Seal the edge with a little egg yolk. Place the finished roll on the prepared tray. Make 11 more spring rolls in the same manner. (You may freeze any remaining wrappers.) The spring rolls may be made 2 hours ahead and chilled, covered with a damp paper towel, or 1 month ahead and frozen. If freezing, freeze rolls on a tray loosely covered with plastic wrap until firm, about 1 hour. Then transfer to heavy-duty sealable plastic bags. Seal the bag, pressing out excess air. Do not thaw before cooking.

To cook the spring rolls, line a plate with two layers of paper towels. In a medium frying or sauté pan, heat the vegetable oil. The oil should be hot enough to make a small chunk of bread sizzle and brown quickly. When the oil is hot, using tongs, gently place the spring rolls in the hot oil. Turn the rolls with tongs so that all sides are crispy and golden brown. When cooked, place on the prepared plate and pat with paper towels to absorb the oil. To serve, divide the Rum-Cider Syrup evenly among six dessert plates. Place two spring rolls on each plate. Sprinkle with powdered sugar and serve with vanilla ice cream.

RUM-CIDER SYRUP

YIELDS 1 CUP

1⅓ cups apple cider
1 teaspoon minced fresh ginger
3 tablespoons corn syrup
3 tablespoons brown sugar
3 tablespoons cold unsalted butter, cut into pieces
1 tablespoon dark rum

In a small saucepan over medium heat, place all the ingredients except the butter and rum. Stir and bring to a boil. Reduce the heat to low and simmer, stirring occasionally, until the mixture is reduced by half, about 35 minutes. Remove the pan from the heat and stir in the butter a few pieces at a time. Whisk in the rum. Serve as directed.

This syrup may be made up to 2 weeks ahead. When cooled, store in the refrigerator in a plastic or glass container. To reheat, pour into a small saucepan and stir occasionally over low heat until warm.

FEBRUARY

A Valentine's Day Dinner for Two

I'm a complete sentimentalist when it comes to Valentine's Day. Ask me to free-associate with February 14 and I'll come up with all the traditional favorites—hearts and lace, chocolates and flowers, Champagne toasts and cheek-to-cheek dancing. Although I think any day's a good time for romance, this is *the* day to indulge in every type of romantic frivolity you can dream up—starting with a totally over-the-top card.

I've always preferred making a card to buying one, partly because people always throw the store-bought ones away. I want what I give to become a keepsake; there's no day like this one for what I call lasting memories. And I know that the more thought I put into my creation, the longer my loved one is going to hold on to it.

The table is dressed up in hot pink with cool apple-green accents. I use candlelight and rose petals to help add romance to the evening, scattering them on the table and throughout the room.

A VALENTINE'S DAY COLLAGE

TIME REQUIRED: 3 to 4 hours

MATERIALS NEEDED

collage elements (see suggestions below)

frame or shadow box from craft or art store

foam craft brushes

craft glue

fabric glue (if you're using fabric)

glue gun (to secure heavier items)

acrylic craft paint

1 Gather collage elements such as ticket stubs, charms, matchbooks, photographs, coins, bottle caps, penny candy, jewelry, ornaments, seashells, old keys. Use all or part of a piece of sheet music, words from a newspaper, a phone book, a map, a train schedule, a perfume or wine label. Gather or buy bits of fabric, lace, or cord, especially anything with texture such as velvet and satin. Check out the clearance section at the fabric stores for small remnants. You can gather odds and ends from anywhere.

2 Find a frame or shadow box (18 to 20 inches) at a craft or art supply store. It should have enough depth to allow you to layer your elements, and be made of a material that can be painted or covered with fabric. In this example, I used velvet.

3 Pick an overall color scheme to help pull the elements together. I'm in a pink mood this year, so I worked with shades of rose and pink, using apple green for accents.

I don't just mean thinking about the person and what he likes. More important, I like to think about things we've experienced together; then I incorporate those shared experiences into what I'm making. I want him to look up at his Valentine's Day card months or years from now and be taken back to the music we heard together when we first met, the time that we spent, the colors of the season, the strawberries that were ripe at that time of year and that he can still almost taste . . . *That's* what I'm aiming for when I make a Valentine's Day keepsake.

You don't need any special skills to put together something that's meaningful, personal, and beautiful—at least, to the two of you. It doesn't even have to be a card. I've always liked the idea of a collage of mementos that you can frame and that can be hung on a wall to be endlessly gazed upon.

To find your collage elements, think about places you've visited together or things you've enjoyed together (the ticket stub from the concert you went to, snapshots from a trip, shells from your day at the beach, sheet music for "your song"); things that will remind him of you—even the parts of you he complains

4 Pick a main element for your collage. The main element in mine is sheet music, made more interesting with a pink color wash. To get the effect, I mixed a small amount of pale pink acrylic paint, about the size of a quarter, with three times as much water, so that the musical score would show through. I used a foam craft brush to apply it.

5 Start to assemble the collage by working on the lining first. If you use fabric, like the shiny satin I chose, you need fabric glue. Allow time for it to dry thoroughly before adding anything else. Another approach would be to staple the fabric to a wooden box frame, then glue felt on top to hide the staples.

6 Take time to play around with the items—move things around, see what fits, and figure out if you'll need any additional elements.

7 Layer the elements to give the collage some dimension. I looped sheer ribbons and draped coordinating fabrics together. Glue the layers in one at a time. Allow each to dry thoroughly before adding new elements, and continue adding until you're happy with the results.

The Valentine's Day collage I gave to Dan captures many of the romantic moments we've shared.

about (a fragment of mirror with a lipstick kiss if he says you spend too much time in the powder room); things you've dreamed of doing together (a magazine picture of a desert island?). Try to use a mixture of two-dimensional and three-dimensional elements to give the collage some depth. Add pieces of fabric and ribbon to fill it out. You just have to use your eye—and your imagination!

You can celebrate love on Valentine's Day in all kinds of ways, from the traditional candlelit dinner to something totally exotic and blissful—just as long as it's inspired and passionate. If you can't arrange to have that romantic Valentine's Day dinner, you might go for breakfast together, which is something that people rarely do unless they're on vacation, or spend the evening having his-and-hers massages—a great prelude to a romantic evening at home.

Since we've been together, Dan and I have spent every Valentine's Day at B. Smith's in New York. Though it's fun being King and Queen of Hearts at the restaurant, we always have our own quiet Valentine's celebration, too. Sometimes I make a special dinner at home. Staying home gives you a chance to exclude the rest of the world and plan the perfect celebration. You can design everything to be a sensual experience, from the moment you're dressed to the last sip of wine or Champagne and the music that ends the evening.

Creating any event at home is like making your own theatrical production: You want to have all the acts in place—the dressed table, memorable foods, a theme, and a finale, too. Creating a Valentine's Day celebration is no different.

This year, I started with my outfit. All year long, I keep my eyes open for the perfect Valentine's Day outfit—the flirtier the better. Once I find it, I hide it away until February 14 arrives. Usually I wear red, which is one of my favorite colors for any occasion. But this year I went for hot pink in a big way. I've always thought of pink as a sensual color, and I like the idea of Valentine's Day being fiery and warm.

Pink set the theme for my decorating, too. I'm an unabashed fan of every over-the-top romantic notion that's ever been dreamed up. This year, I used unscented candles and pink roses to transform our dining alcove into a romantic niche; and I scattered pink rose petals in strategic spots—the foyer, under the glass plates, all over the table, and along the floor in a pink path to the bedroom, where scented candles, fragrant oils and massages, satiny lingerie, and more rose petals awaited us.

I've learned how important it is to add little touches to the table that pick up on the theme of the occasion. Though my everyday style is handsome and womanly, there's also a girlish side of me that likes lace and frills; this side comes out on Valentine's Day. So for my tablecloth, in contrast with the sexy pink of my outfit, I chose a soft, girlish pink, with added touches here and there of several other shades of pink. I used apple-green napkins to pick up on the green I used in my Valentine's Day collage. Thus I married two colors I happen to love together.

I planned a Valentine's Day menu that's delicious, luxurious, light, easy, and sensual. Dining in the spirit of *l'amour* calls for a meal that's delicate, not hearty, and a little out of the ordinary. And it should require very little last-minute fussing. You won't inspire romantic thoughts when you're hovering over the stove wearing oven mitts.

The little heart-shaped bundles of swordfish in parchment that I prepared ahead of time and stored in the refrigerator just needed to be brought to room temperature and popped in the oven. And what could be more appropriate for Valentine's Day than a dish that can't be enjoyed until the wrapping is peeled off?

Think about your partner and what he enjoys eating—even if it's meatloaf and mashed potatoes. It might be nice to serve his absolute favorite. Also think about what would be an exciting start to the meal. Dan and I both like vodka and oysters, so oyster shooters with caviar is the perfect appetizer.

While we dined on oysters, which I had also prepared in advance, a crab soufflé for two was rising in the oven. I thought it would be nice to have something for us to dip into together. Sharing food from the same container can be a sensual experience.

You have to have chocolate on Valentine's Day. I went for *triple* chocolate torte, with a pistachio sauce and pink sugared flower petals as a garnish. Even if you opt for a store-bought cake or dessert, you could make or buy the flowers to garnish it.

The morning after, keep the sizzle going with flambéed breakfast crêpes and other treats. Have the breakfast tray ready, set with pretty china and a bud vase. The crêpes, along with blood oranges marinated in Grand Marnier, doused with rum, and set aflame, make for a luxurious start to the day.

Like any celebration, Valentine's Day gives us an opportunity to do things we don't normally do. Not only do we get to surround ourselves with flowers and Champagne and sensual foods; we also get the chance to make good on promises to a loved one that we didn't keep, or to woo somebody that we've had a crush on for the longest time. It's an occasion for taking liberties you wouldn't normally take, in the name of love. And the best thing about love is that you don't even have to wait until February 14 rolls around to celebrate it. You can plan a weekend of endless romance anytime, and there's no better way to get started than with a sensual meal.

A Valentine's Day Dinner for Two

Pepper Vodka Oyster Shooters
with Caviar

—

Crab Soufflé with Toast Points Pour Deux

—

Heart-Shaped Swordfish Papillotes
with Mango Salsa

Triple Chocolate Torte
with Pistachio Sauce and
Sugared Flower Petals

—

Chardonnay, Jordan, Alexander Valley, 1996
(or any other Chardonnay)

Moët & Chandon, Brut Impérial, 1993
(or any other Champagne)

*Pepper Vodka Oyster
Shooters with Caviar*

PEPPER VODKA OYSTER SHOOTERS WITH CAVIAR

SERVES 2

2 ounces pepper vodka, chilled
2 medium raw oysters
2 teaspoons cocktail sauce
¼ teaspoon black caviar

Into each of two shot glasses, pour 1 once chilled pepper vodka. Add an oyster, 1 teaspoon cocktail sauce, and ⅛ teaspoon caviar to each glass.

CRAB SOUFFLÉ WITH TOAST POINTS POUR DEUX

SERVES 2

¾ cup mayonnaise
2 tablespoons chopped scallions
(2 to 3 scallions)
2 tablespoons fresh-squeezed lemon juice
¼ teaspoon cayenne pepper
¾ teaspoon Old Bay Seasoning
1¼ cups fresh lump crabmeat
2 egg whites, beaten stiff
4 toast points

Preheat the oven to 400 degrees. Place the rack in the center of the oven. Butter one 2-cup soufflé dish or two 1-cup soufflé dishes. In a medium bowl, combine the mayonnaise, scallions, lemon juice, pepper, and Old Bay Seasoning. Set aside.

Pick through and clean crabmeat making sure there are no shells. Stir the crabmeat into the mayonnaise mixture until just combined; do not overmix.

With a rubber spatula, gently fold the beaten egg whites into the mayonnaise mixture.

Spoon into soufflé dish(es). The soufflé will fill the dish all the way to the top. Place the dish(es) on a baking sheet on the center rack of the oven. Bake until firm and fluffy golden brown, 8 to 10 minutes for a 1-cup soufflé, 15 to 18 minutes for a 2-cup soufflé. Serve immediately with toast points.

HEART-SHAPED SWORDFISH PAPILLOTES with MANGO SALSA

SERVES 2

*Two 8-ounce swordfish fillets,
all skin removed*

1 tablespoon olive oil

½ medium plantain, peeled and julienned

*1 medium or 2 small carrots, peeled and
julienned*

½ medium zucchini, julienned

1 medium tomato, seeded and julienned

*2 tablespoons jerk sauce (store-bought—
Vernon's, Walker's, Wood, etc.)*

*1½ cups diced fresh, frozen, or canned
mango (¼-inch dice)*

Salt and freshly ground black pepper to taste

1 tablespoon butter, melted

Fresh thyme sprigs for garnish

Mango Salsa (recipe follows)

Rinse the fillets in cold water and pat dry. Preheat the oven to 400 degrees. On a clean dry work surface, fold a piece of parchment about 16 inches long in half. Cut half a heart shape with the fold in the center so that when the paper is opened, you have a full heart shape. Repeat. Place the parchment hearts on a baking sheet. Brush the surfaces of the hearts with olive oil. On the right half of each heart, place half of the plantains and one fourth of the carrots, zucchini, and tomato. Brush each fillet with jerk sauce on both sides. Place the fillets on top of the vegetables. Sprinkle the mango equally over each fillet. Lay the remaining julienned vegetables over the fillets. Sprinkle lightly with salt and pepper. Fold the left half of the parchment heart over the fish and, starting from the top of the heart, fold the paper over itself, creasing and rolling until you come to the point of the heart. Twist the point tightly to secure the pouch. Brush the parchment with butter. Bake 10 minutes. Remove from the oven. Let stand 1 minute. Lift the pouch at the corners and place on a plate. Slice along the curved edge with a sharp knife and lift the paper to reveal the swordfish. Garnish with thyme sprigs and serve immediately with Mango Salsa.

MANGO SALSA

1 cup fresh, frozen, or canned diced mango

¼ cup diced red bell pepper (¼-inch dice)

1 scallion, finely chopped

2 tablespoons chopped fresh cilantro

Juice of 1 lime

2 teaspoons olive oil

Salt and freshly ground black pepper to taste

Combine all the ingredients in a small bowl. Toss until mixed. Chill. Serve alongside Swordfish Papillotes.

TRIPLE CHOCOLATE TORTE WITH PISTACHIO SAUCE AND SUGARED FLOWER PETALS

This rich chocolate torte should be made a day in advance. Since the torte yields sixteen slices, you can serve it at your Valentine's Day dinner and then refrigerate the remainder (for up to a week). That way you can indulge in several post–Valentine's Day desserts.   **ONE 10-INCH TORTE**

1¾ cups (3½ sticks) unsalted butter

1¼ pounds semisweet chocolate

6 tablespoons strong brewed coffee

3 tablespoons Kahlúa or other coffee-flavored liqueur

2½ cups sugar

10 large eggs

Pistachio Sauce (recipe follows)

Sugared Flower Petals (recipe follows)

To prepare the 10-inch springform pan, butter the pan thoroughly. Cut three pieces of aluminum foil approximately 12 × 17 inches each. On a clean dry work surface, place two sheets on top of one another to form a cross. Place the pan in the center and wrap the outside of the pan firmly with the foil, rolling down the top edges, keeping the foil on the outside of the pan. This is to keep the bottom of the pan sealed extra tight. Set the pan and remaining sheet of foil aside.

Preheat the oven to 350 degrees. Place the rack in the center of the oven. In a heavy 2-quart saucepan or double boiler over low heat, melt the butter and chocolate. Stir often to prevent the chocolate from burning. Remove from the heat. Add the coffee and Kahlúa. Set aside.

In the large bowl of an electric mixer or by hand with a wire whisk, beat the sugar and eggs until well blended. Pour the chocolate into the egg mixture. Whisk the batter until all the ingredients are combined. Pour the batter into the prepared pan and cover tightly with the remaining sheet of foil.

Place a large baking pan or cookie sheet with 2-inch sides, large enough to accommodate the springform pan, on the center rack of the oven. Place the torte in the pan. Fill the baking pan with water that comes one quarter of the way up the sides of the torte pan. Using the tip of a sharp knife, poke three nickel-size holes into the foil covering the torte. Bake for 2 hours and 20 minutes, checking occasionally to add water if needed to maintain depth.

Carefully remove the torte from the water bath. Remove the foil cover. Let cool on a rack for about 2 hours. Cover with plastic wrap and refrigerate overnight.

To unmold the torte, dampen a sponge or kitchen towel with warm water. Rub around the outside of the pan. Gently unlatch the sides and pull away from the torte. To remove the pan bottom, place a piece of plastic wrap over the top surface of the torte. Place a cookie sheet on top of the torte and turn it over so that the torte is upside down. With a warm, damp sponge, gently rub the pan bottom. Place your chosen cake plate or platter on the torte and turn it upside down again. Lift off the cookie sheet and remove the plastic wrap. Pool pistachio sauce around the base of the cake, and decorate with sugared flower petals, if desired.

PISTACHIO SAUCE

¾ cup unsalted, shelled pistachios
2 egg yolks
½ cup sugar
1½ cups milk
1 teaspoon vanilla extract
2 tablespoons Cointreau

Preheat the oven to 400 degrees. Spread the pistachios on a baking sheet in a single layer. Roast in the oven 4 minutes. Allow to cool. In a food processor or nut grinder, grind the cooled nuts very fine. Set aside.

In a medium bowl, whisk the egg yolks and sugar together. The mixture will be very thick, almost a paste. Set aside. In a heavy medium saucepan over medium heat, cook the milk and vanilla, stirring often with a wooden spoon or wire whisk until bubbles form around the edges of the pan. Reduce the heat to low. Pour 1 cup of the warm milk mixture slowly into the yolk mixture, whisking constantly until smooth. Return this mixture to the saucepan. Cook the custard over medium heat, whisking constantly, until thickened, about 2 to 3 minutes. Do not allow to boil. Remove from the heat. Whisk in the Cointreau and ground pistachios. Cool. Cover and refrigerate until ready to use.

NOTE: Custard will thicken slightly when cooled. Ultimately, the custard should be a little thicker than heavy cream. If the custard is too thick when cool, whisk in a little cream or half-and-half. If desired, substitute other liqueurs for the Cointreau. You might try Drambuie or a pistachio liqueur.

SUGARED FLOWER PETALS

Rose petals, violets, and other edible flowers (see Note)

1 egg white

Extrafine granulated sugar

In a small bowl, beat the egg white with a fork until light but not frothy. Pour some sugar into another small bowl. Line a cookie sheet with waxed paper. Place a baking rack on another cookie sheet. Set aside.

Holding the base of a flower or a petal with tweezers, gently paint or dab egg white on all sides and surfaces, using a small, good-quality paintbrush. Or dip the flower or petal in the egg white, dabbing with the paintbrush to cover any missed areas. Gently shake off excess egg white.

Hold the flower or petal over the cookie sheet lined with waxed paper, and with spoon or sieve, gently dust sugar over the flower or petal, turning as needed to coat all surfaces. If you miss a spot, gently dab on more egg white and sprinkle with a little more sugar.

As each flower or petal is sugared, place it on the baking rack and allow to dry in a dry, airy spot for at least 1 hour. Store uncovered and exposed to air at all times. Your flowers will keep for 2 to 3 days in a dry environment.

In addition to the Triple Chocolate Torte, you can use these flowers to decorate other cakes, desserts, and homemade chocolates.

NOTE: While many flowers besides roses and violets are edible—among them pansies, lilacs, and carnations—some flowers are poisonous. Please make certain that a flower is safe before using it in this recipe!

A MARDI GRAS BUFFET

Even though I've lived all my life in the United States, I didn't discover Carnival until I went to Vienna as a young model. There, just as in New Orleans, February is a time of Carnival balls and parties surrounding a fantastic Carnival parade. All of that was rather enticing to me, so when I came back to the States I explored Carnival some more. And in doing so, I discovered New Orleans, a city with a spirit as spicy as its food.

Mardi Gras has all the feistiness of New Orleans, with all of the city's diverse influences. Carnival here is influenced by Caribbean, African, French, English, and Native American culture; it's a big melting-pot experience—and out of it grows all the spirited colors and foods and music and dancing and costumes that make Mardi Gras the truly spectacular event that it is.

My Mardi Gras buffet is inspired by the New Orleans Carnival, which is a wildly festive, anything-goes type of celebration culminating on the eve of Ash Wednesday. The next day, Lent begins. My own version of the celebration has all the flavors and colors of Mardi Gras without the forty days of abstinence.

Mardi Gras reveling was brought to New Orleans in the early nineteenth century by some returning Creoles, who were as excited by the festivities they'd witnessed in Paris as I was by the Viennese Carnival. His Majesty Rex, King of the Carnival, first proclaimed it an official holiday in New Orleans in 1872. All the masked revelers joined a single pro-cession—the first daytime Mardi Gras parade—and purple, green, and gold were chosen as the holiday colors. Each color has a symbolic meaning:

For Mardi Gras I like to pull out all the stops. Color adds rhythm, so the more color, the better. It's a time to dance, play, and have fun.

Gold is for power, green for faith, and purple for justice. I use all three as the basis for my own Mardi Gras decorations.

The first New Orleans krewe, or Carnival club, called itself "The Mystik Krewe of Comus" and built two floats to parade by torchlight. Nowadays there are numerous krewes, each with its own exotic name. They hold parades throughout the eleven days and nights preceding Mardi Gras. A king and queen of each krewe rides on a float along with other masked and costumed merrymakers, and toss the crowd trinkets—anything from specially minted coins to beads, garters, Moon Pies, and the occasional bag of peanuts! There's something uniquely Carnival-like about these funky, colorful trinkets, so I make sure to pick up on the theme when I decorate.

Along with the parades, dozens of krewe balls are held during the Mardi Gras season. And all of this is just a prelude to the Grand Parade on Mardi Gras Day, when thousands of people in costumes of every sort ride on floats and parade through the streets.

At B. Smith's in New York, we cook up a special event to celebrate Mardi Gras, with our own masked ball. Our friends and customers make up a kind of "New York krewe," a varied mix of people of every age, profession, and ethnic group. I believe that merrymaking on the scale of Mardi Gras is for the kids as well as the adults, so when my stepdaughter, Dana, was still small, we started a tradition of making this a family celebration. I always felt it was important to create a kind of extended family for her since she doesn't have relatives living nearby. We would invite her friends from school and their parents, and we'd dance and have contests for the best costume and the best dancers—all in fun.

Even when we celebrate Mardi Gras at home, people get into that sense of theater. I think everyone enjoys dressing with a theme in mind; it creates a bit of excitement before you even get to where you're going. And when you're in costume, you're ready to party, so all it takes is some lively music—anything from the Neville Brothers to Dixieland—to get people out on the dance floor. You *have* to have dance music at a Mardi Gras celebration.

This year, I put together a funky little outfit in all the stripes and colors of Mardi Gras and wore a feathery mask. And I used the same theme, based on the

Experiment with fun patterns, masks, and bold table settings, including colorful plates, napkins, and silverware, which add to the festivity.

Mardi Gras colors but certainly not limited to them, to decorate my home. Around Christmastime I had come across some beautiful, Harlequin-patterned glass ornaments designed by Christopher Radko, who's done trees for the White House. The moment I saw them, I knew they'd be perfect for dressing up my Mardi Gras buffet table. Regular Christmas ornaments—solid-colored gold, green, and purple ones if you want to keep the color symbolism—would look great, too. It's just a matter of using whatever you can find to create your own interpretation of this glorious celebration of excess. When people come in and see the festiveness of the table setting and the food, they're immediately in the spirit of Mardi Gras.

I also had found some bright, checkered wrapping paper right before Christmas. I liked the colors, so I bought it. I never ended up using it for Christmas, but when Mardi Gras came around I pulled it out of the closet and spread it over my kitchen island. That's how I work: I'll buy or save things just because I really love them, even if I don't know what I'm going to do with them. When it's time to get creative with a holiday environment, I have a whole collection of papers and fabrics and intriguing objects to choose from.

Especially for Mardi Gras, I liked the juxtaposition of the very festive ornaments with the regal, dark green velvet I found in my closet and used to cover the buffet table. I put out yellow, green, and purple plates, flatware with colorful handles, and three colors of napkins (I chose paper napkins because they come in such bright hues, and tied them with funky little Mardi Gras–colored beads). For that final Carnival-trinket touch, I scattered coins and beads around, brought out some masks I'd kept from previous years (you or your kids could easily make some with colored paper and sequins) and topped it all off with pink feathers and a fiery pink feather boa.

Mardi Gras isn't just a visual feast. One of the great things about the event is that it appeals to all of the senses—not least the sense of taste. In fact, the holiday is really one long excuse to indulge to the very limit before the forty-day period of abstinence begins. The feasting kicks off at the stroke of midnight and continues until Easter Sunday.

My Mardi Gras menu is heavily inspired by Louisiana traditions, which in turn are shaped by that melting pot of cultures that makes up New Orleans and gave rise to Creole and Cajun cooking. French and Spanish colonists created Creole dishes by adapting their traditional recipes to local ingredients: When they added shrimp and crab from the Gulf of Mexico to the French fish stew known as bouillabaisse, the result was gumbo; and Spanish paella became jambalaya.

Along with mildly spicy Creole red beans, I serve two classic Louisiana dishes on Mardi Gras: a multicolored shrimp maque choux (mine combines yellow corn, red tomatoes, green bell pepper, and pink shrimp) and a gumbo with chicken, sausage, and okra. My menu also includes some Cajun dishes, which are more earthy, hotter and spicier than the Creole: the oyster salad on the menu, my own version of a Cajun dish, is one of my favorites—I love the unusual combination of the warm oysters against the crispy salad greens, with the spicy vinaigrette. I serve the meal with a Champagne punch in which I float deep red strawberries.

This Mardi Gras meal, with the corn, shrimp, beans, and chicken, has enough sustenance to get anyone through a Lenten fast. And that's not counting dessert— a coconut bread pudding with a bourbon crème anglaise, and King's Cake.

King Cake is a Carnival staple, going back to the 1800s. It's a lot of fun, because you frost it with a thin icing and then sprinkle it with sugars in all the colors of Mardi Gras. The cake—a braided yeast cake you can even make in a bread machine—is served at krewe balls at the stroke of midnight, along with a glass of Champagne punch. What's special about it is the favor you might find baked into your piece. A century ago, young unmarried men and women would share a beautifully decorated cake that had a pea on one side and a bean on the other. Ladies were served from the pea side, men from the bean side, and whoever found the pea and bean became king and queen for the night. Today, favors are still baked into the cake. If you bite into a bean, a pecan, or a plastic baby charm, you become the king or queen of your party.

A Mardi Gras Buffet for Twelve

Oyster Po' Boy Salad with
Spicy Cajun Vinaigrette

Shrimp Maque Choux

Chicken, Sausage, and Okra Gumbo

Creole Red Beans

Coconut Bread Pudding
with Bourbon Crème Anglaise

King Cake

Creole Punch

Steamed Rice
French Quarter café
Maker's Mark bourbon

Petite Syrah, Foppiano, Russian River, 1993 (or any other Syrah)

Mardi Gras is a time to indulge. Guests feast on (clockwise from top)
Oyster Po' Boy Salad with Spicy Cajun Vinaigrette, Shrimp Maque
Choux, Creole Red Beans, and Chicken, Sausage, and Okra Gumbo.

OYSTER PO' BOY SALAD WITH SPICY CAJUN VINAIGRETTE

SERVES 12

3 dozen oysters, shucked

1½ cups all-purpose flour

1½ tablespoons dried thyme leaves

1 teaspoon salt

¾ teaspoon freshly ground black pepper

¼ teaspoon cayenne pepper

1 cup vegetable oil

12 cups mixed baby greens, washed and dried

Spicy Cajun Vinaigrette (recipe follows)

12 to 24 slices toasted French bread

Drain the oysters and pat dry with paper towels. Stir together the flour, thyme, salt, black pepper, and cayenne pepper on a plate. In a skillet over medium-high heat, heat the oil. Dredge each oyster in the seasoned flour, shaking off excess. Set aside on a piece of waxed paper. Cook the oysters in batches, 1 to 2 minutes on each side until golden brown. Don't overcrowd the pan and don't overcook the oysters. Drain on a brown-paper-covered rack.

In a large salad bowl, toss the mixed baby greens with the Spicy Cajun Vinaigrette. Add the fried oysters and toss. Arrange the toasted French bread slices around the edge of the bowl and serve immediately.

SPICY CAJUN VINAIGRETTE

3 tablespoons fresh-squeezed lemon juice

2 tablespoons balsamic vinegar

1 tablespoon Dijon mustard

2 cloves garlic

2 teaspoons Worcestershire sauce

¼ to ½ teaspoon Tabasco sauce

Salt and freshly ground black pepper to taste

⅔ cup extra virgin olive oil

In a blender, puree the lemon juice, vinegar, mustard, garlic, Worcestershire sauce, Tabasco sauce, salt, and pepper. Slowly add the olive oil in a thin stream while blending.

SHRIMP MAQUE CHOUX

SERVES 12

5 tablespoons unsalted butter

1¼ cups chopped onions

1¼ cups chopped green bell peppers

½ cup fish stock or clam juice

5½ cups fresh or thawed frozen corn kernels

4 cups chopped plum tomatoes

1 teaspoon salt

¾ teaspoon ground white pepper

¼ teaspoon hot paprika

1½ pounds cooked, peeled, and deveined baby shrimp, thawed if frozen

1 cup sliced scallions

In a large skillet or sauté pan over medium-high heat, melt the butter. Add the onions and bell peppers, and sauté 4 to 5 minutes until softened. Stir in the fish stock, corn, tomatoes, salt, white pepper, and paprika. Reduce the heat to medium and cook 10 minutes, stirring occasionally. Add the shrimp and continue cooking 5 to 10 minutes until the vegetables are cooked and the shrimp is heated through. Sprinkle with the sliced scallions to serve.

CHICKEN, SAUSAGE, AND OKRA GUMBO

SERVES 12

2 tablespoons olive oil

1½ pounds skinned and boned chicken, cut in 1½- to 2-inch pieces

12 ounces andouille or kielbasa sausage, sliced into ½-inch pieces

2 cups chopped onions

1½ cups chopped green bell peppers

1½ cups chopped celery

3 cloves garlic, minced

1 pound okra, trimmed and cut into 1-inch pieces

3 cups chopped, peeled, and seeded tomatoes

(continued)

In a large pot or Dutch oven, heat the olive oil. Add the chicken and sausage, and cook over medium-high heat 5 minutes. Add the onions, bell peppers, celery, and garlic to the pot and cook 6 to 7 minutes, stirring often, until the onions are transparent. Stir in the okra, tomatoes, chicken stock, bay leaves, paprika, basil, thyme, and salt. Bring to a boil, reduce heat, and simmer, partially covered, 30 minutes, until the okra is tender and gumbo is slightly thickened.

3 cups chicken stock

4 bay leaves

1 tablespoon hot paprika

2 teaspoons dried basil leaves

2 teaspoons dried thyme leaves

1½ teaspoons salt

½ cup chopped parsley

The gumbo may be made ahead, cooled, and refrigerated overnight. Reheat gently on top of the stove. Remove the bay leaves and sprinkle the gumbo with the chopped parsley before serving with steamed rice.

CREOLE RED BEANS

SERVES 12

3 tablespoons olive oil

2 cups chopped onions

3 cloves garlic, minced

1½ cups chopped celery

1½ cups chopped carrots

¾ cup chopped red bell pepper

¾ cup chopped green bell pepper

1 or 2 jalapeño peppers, seeded and chopped

2 teaspoons dried thyme leaves

2 teaspoons dried basil leaves

2 teaspoons dried oregano leaves

1½ teaspoons ground cumin

1 tablespoon hot paprika

1½ teaspoons salt

1½ cups chicken stock

Three 15-ounce cans kidney beans, drained, or 4½ cups cooked beans

One 28-ounce can whole tomatoes, drained and chopped

Salt and freshly ground black pepper to taste

In a large saucepan over medium-high heat, heat the oil. Sauté the onions and garlic until softened, about 3 minutes. Add the celery, carrots, bell peppers, jalapeño peppers, thyme, basil, oregano, cumin, paprika, and 1½ teaspoons salt. Cook 5 to 10 minutes, stirring in the chicken stock to prevent sticking. When the vegetables are tender, stir in the kidney beans and tomatoes. Reduce the heat and simmer 20 to 30 minutes, or until the beans are tender. Add salt and pepper to taste. Remove from the stove and pour the beans into a heated serving bowl with a cover.

COCONUT BREAD PUDDING WITH BOURBON CRÈME ANGLAISE

SERVES 12

4 cups cubed stale French bread, crusts removed (1-inch cubes)

1½ cups sweetened shredded coconut

1 cup sugar

1½ cups heavy cream

½ cup coconut cream, canned

3 large eggs, lightly beaten

2 tablespoons melted butter

1 teaspoon vanilla or coconut extract

2 tablespoons bourbon

Bourbon Crème Anglaise (recipe follows)

Preheat the oven to 350 degrees. Butter a loaf pan or 2-quart baking dish.

In a large bowl, stir together the bread cubes, coconut, and sugar. In a medium bowl, whisk together the remaining ingredients; pour over the dry ingredients and stir until blended. Pour into the prepared pan. Bake 45 to 50 minutes, until golden brown and a knife inserted in the center comes out clean. Serve the pudding with a small pitcher of Bourbon Crème Anglaise.

BOURBON CRÈME ANGLAISE

YIELDS 2¼ CUPS

1½ cups heavy cream

½ cup half-and-half

½ cup sugar, divided

6 large egg yolks

2½ teaspoons vanilla extract

2 tablespoons bourbon

In a double boiler over medium heat, heat the cream, half-and-half, and ¼ cup of the sugar, until just simmering. Whisk together the egg yolks, remaining sugar, and vanilla in a medium bowl. Slowly whisk one cup of the warm cream mixture into the yolk mixture. After combining, add the yolk mixture and bourbon to the remaining cream mixture. Stir continuously until the mixture thickens, about 6 to 8 minutes. Cool 25 minutes and strain over a medium bowl. Refrigerate until ready to serve.

KING CAKE

You'll need to start this recipe a day ahead of time, since the dough must be chilled overnight. SERVES 12–15

CAKE

¾ cup warm milk (105–115 degrees)

1 package active dry yeast

⅔ cup granulated sugar, divided

1 teaspoon grated orange peel

½ teaspoon salt

½ teaspoon ground mace

¾ cup (1½ sticks) softened unsalted butter

4 large eggs

4 cups all-purpose flour

1½ teaspoons ground cinnamon

1 dried bean or plastic baby charm

TOPPING

2 cups powdered sugar

½ teaspoon orange or vanilla extract

4 to 5 tablespoons milk

3 tablespoons each yellow, green, and purple decorating sugar

To make the cake, in the large bowl of an electric mixer, sprinkle the yeast over the milk. Stir until dissolved. Stir in 6 tablespoons of the granulated sugar, the orange peel, salt, mace, butter, and eggs. Add 3 cups of the flour; beat at medium speed 4 minutes. Add the remaining flour; beat at low speed until smooth—about 2 minutes.

Cover the bowl with oiled plastic wrap; let rise in a warm, draft-free place until doubled in bulk—about 1 hour. Refrigerate, covered, overnight.

In a small bowl, combine the remaining sugar and the cinnamon. Set aside. Punch down the dough, it will be soft. Working quickly, divide the dough into three equal pieces. Roll one dough piece into a rectangle approximately 24 × 6 inches; sprinkle one third of the cinnamon-sugar mixture over the rectangle. Starting on a long side, roll the dough into a cylinder, pinching the edges together to seal. Repeat with the remaining dough pieces. Place the rolls side by side; braid loosely. Gently transfer the braid to a parchment-lined baking sheet; shape into an oval, pinching the ends together to seal. Cover with a clean towel; let rise in warm place 45 minutes.

Preheat oven to 375 degrees. Bake 25 to 30 minutes, until golden brown. Cool on a wire rack. Insert the bean or charm into the cake from the bottom. (Please be sure to remind guests that they should be careful not to swallow the charm, and that parents should watch small children closely when they are eating the cake.)

To make the topping, in a medium bowl, combine the powdered sugar, orange extract, and milk. Beat with a wooden spoon until smooth. Spread on the top of the cooled cake. Spoon the colored sugars on top of the icing in wide bands, alternating purple, green, and yellow.

NOTE: King Cake dough may be made in a bread machine by combining the milk, butter, eggs, 6 tablespoons sugar, orange peel, salt, mace, flour, and yeast in the pan according to the manufacturer's instructions. Set the machine for the dough cycle. When ready, refrigerate the dough overnight in a greased sealable plastic bag. Proceed with the directions above for shaping, baking, and decorating the cake.

CREOLE PUNCH

SERVES 12

1 cup brandy
1 quart cranberry juice
1 quart orange juice
One 25.4-ounce bottle Champagne
One 25.4-ounce bottle sparkling cider
1 quart strawberries, hulled and halved

Mix the brandy and cranberry and orange juices together. Refrigerate until ready to serve. Pour the mixture into a large punch bowl, and just before serving add the Champagne, sparkling cider, and strawberries. Serve over ice.

MARCH

DANA'S RITE-OF-PASSAGE DINNER

March is a month of change and growth. It is also Women's History Month, which focuses on the strides made by strong women. So March seemed just the right time of year to have a celebration in honor of my stepdaughter, Dana's, entry into her teen years. I believe that it's important in every girl's life to mark her first step toward becoming a grown woman with a joyful rite of passage.

When you mark a person's movement from one phase of life to another with ritual and celebration, you ease the passage. People all over the world and through history have had rites to celebrate major life changes—coming of age, marriage, becoming a mother, and even the naming of babies. It's a way of acknowledging that this person is about to be reborn as someone new. You want to prepare her for her new life so that she'll feel positive about what's coming, and confident that she'll become everything you hope she can be.

For Dana's Rite-of-Passage Dinner I used an African theme. The table is covered with mud cloth and the centerpiece features gourds in the shape of animals. I put out plenty of homemade Plantain and Sweet Potato Chips before dinner is served.

Some of the celebrations we have today are rites of passage, even if we don't think of them that way—christenings and baby showers, graduations from grade school, and so on. And, though some of us have forgotten these traditional rites of passage, people are now inventing brand-new ones for times in their lives that they feel are turning points, and about which they may be apprehensive.

A friend of mine created a rite of passage for her fiftieth birthday: She had a weekend pajama party with her friends at a local hotel. You could have one for that fortieth birthday, when many of us feel we're leaving our youth behind, or for a seventy-fifth. People I know have had rites for a second wedding. You could have a rite of passage for your child *and* yourself when your child leaves home for college or her first apartment; it's a good way to look forward to new possibilities instead of an empty nest. Retirement—truly a rebirth—is another change to celebrate. You've had a life of doing things one way. Now you're starting a new life of doing things you want to do, your way and at your pace.

But the most important rite of passage has always been that of the child becoming an adult. Traditionally, it focused the young person on a life ahead that would follow the same pattern as generations of lives preceding: The boy would take on his father's role; the girl would become a wife and mother. This being the nineties, I had something a little different in mind for Dana. I wanted to support her in becoming the best female human being she can become, and that meant letting her know that in today's world, she can become anything. I also wanted her to be aware of the strides women have made in the last century—not to take for granted the options she has. And, especially at an age when a lot of girls start to lose their self-confidence, I wanted her to know that she has the strength to help break new ground for women.

I had big ideas for Dana's coming of age, but she told me she didn't think her twelfth birthday would be anything special. "Once you've reached double digits, another one is no big deal," she announced. Nevertheless, she did have some expectations for her birthday celebration. We agreed that she could have a party with her friends on her actual birthday, and another, different sort of event in March that would involve mostly family and grownups.

It just so happened that this year, Dana was studying genealogy in school and preparing a family tree that included biographies of her parents. She did a page on her mother, and one on her father and me. The exercise helped inspire Dana to think about who she is and where she came from—and that's what the events I planned for her were all about.

Traditionally, a rite of passage involves a period of preparation with the elders followed by a big celebration with plenty of feasting and dancing, as well as story-telling and the giving of gifts. I created two events for Dana based on the same principles. The first event, a ladies-only brunch with the women who had been most important in her life, was a way of preparing her for the new phase in her life; the second, a big party later that day with family and friends, was the celebration.

I encourage Dana to take pride in the fact that she is descended from two cultures—African American and Blackfoot Indian—and that both acknowledged young women's passages into adulthood with special rituals. Both the events I had in mind were modern rites that would help her honor her past and look forward to her future. The idea was to have the most important people in her world acknowledge what was unique about her, and what was so significant about this moment when she was stepping onto the threshold of adult life.

I thought a morning spent with women who had known Dana since early childhood, reminiscing about her childhood and about our adolescent years, would be a wonderful way to prepare Dana for her step into adulthood and the evening rituals. And what better way to do it than over a relaxed brunch?

I sent out invitations accompanied by T-shirts that I printed with some pas-sages from *Just Us Women,* a book that had special significance for Dana and me. When Dana was small, she loved to have me read her this story of an aunt and her young niece traveling south together by convertible. Anytime Dana and I had a private expedition planned and Dan would ask to come along, Dana and I would exchange smiles as she said, "No, Dad, you can't. This is for *just us women.*"

I like to pull out all the stops on celebration days. That doesn't necessarily mean making things complicated, but it does mean doing everything with flair. So when I decided to serve pancakes at the brunch, I was determined to serve them in a way that made them extraspecial. I decided to "accessorize" them: After all, the idea of "accessories" is truly a woman thing.

I served the pancakes together with two pitchers of syrup. One held Dana's new favorite flavor, strawberry, and in the other was praline, which happens to be

T-SHIRT INVITATION

We created the T-shirts that were part of our invitation package using a photo-transfer technique.

TIME REQUIRED: 1 hour

MATERIALS

image to transfer

photo transfer paper (available at craft stores)

access to a copy machine

white T-Shirt

teflon-covered ironing board

iron

1 Select an image and text you want to use on the shirt. (We got permission to reproduce our image from HarperCollins, formerly Harper & Row, which published *Just Us Women* in 1982. The book was written by Jeannette Caines and illustrated by Pat Cummings.)

2 Using a regular or color copier, enlarge or reduce the image until it is the exact size you want.

3 Have the artwork photocopied onto transfer paper, to produce a mirror image. Be sure to read carefully the manufacturer's instructions, and note that transfer paper prints on one side only. (Make sure that it is inserted correctly into the copier paper tray.)

4 Once you have the image on transfer paper, transfer it to the T-shirt: Place the iron on the hottest setting (usually the linen setting), making sure that the iron is free of all water or steam. Place the T-shirt on the ironing board and run the iron over the area where you will place the image. While the shirt is still hot, place the transfer on it, face down. To initiate the bond, run the iron lightly over the entire image. Repeat, using heavier strokes, for about one minute. Be sure to cover all the edges. To remove the transfer paper, reheat the entire surface with the iron, then, starting in one corner, immediately peel off the paper.

a favorite of mine. In addition, I set out bowls of chopped nuts, chocolate chips, and berries, and as the icing on the cake, so to speak, bowls filled with clouds of spiced whipped cream to heap on top. I kept the beverages simple—just cappuccino and cold, fresh milk.

Like the menu, our conversation was both down-to-earth and sweet. I told my guests that they could consider Dana their "initiate." Every young woman needs guides and advisors as she moves into and through adulthood, and I hoped these women would fill that role for Dana. We told stories about Dana's younger days—some of the fun things she did when she was little, the energy she had when she was just a tot. And we reminisced—and laughed—about our own growing pains during adolescence. When a twelve-year-old hears someone like a mother or aunt speak to her about the crushes she had when *she* was a teen, it validates the girl's own new and unfamiliar feelings and tells her that it's okay to fall for someone.

To honor Dana on this day, we gave her some carefully chosen gifts. Mine were two remembrance pillows I had made out of brightly colored dresses she had worn as a little girl. I had saved them mainly because seeing her in them had meant so much to me. But I knew that one day they'd mean a lot to Dana, too. Over the years, we grow to cherish certain things from our childhood. They form the thread of who we are, give our lives stability, and help us move forward.

So, before Dana's birthday, I cut the dress fabric into quilting squares, added ribbons, and made pillows that could adorn her bed during her teen years, comfort her during her college days, and, as a cherished heirloom in the years to come, would help her bring her past along with her.

Along with the pillows, other gifts came from our guests and me, all meant to make Dana feel feminine: hair ornaments, sweet-smelling lotions and perfumes, nail polish, pretty lingerie, and a long dress to wear to her party that evening.

For the evening celebration, the men joined the party, along with close friends and family members Dana's age. It was a time for everyone to share in the happiness of the moment with feasting and talk, plus music and dance. I also wanted the party to conjure up Dana's distant ancestry in a fun way, at the same time as it celebrated her entry into the rhythm of her adolescent years. So I designed the event around dancing and drums, and, in decorating for the party, I played with a safari theme.

A lively animal fabric print from Africa that hangs in our family room gave me something to work around. For a centerpiece, I used some African gourds in the shape of animals with bobbing heads, along with

I couldn't bear to part with the dresses Dana wore as a little girl, so I sewed a few of them for remembrance pillows—something Dana could hold on to as a keepsake for years to come.

MEMORY BOOK

You can make a memory book for a coming-of-age party or as a keepsake for any special event. Use fabrics, beads, trimmings, markers, paint, and your imagination to decorate the cover and the pages.

TIME REQUIRED: 2 to 3 hours

MATERIALS

handmade paper (from art supply, craft, or stationery supply shop)

ready-made scrapbook or medium-weight cardboard

hole punch

glitter glue pen or metallic marker

grommet kit (from hardware store)

ribbon

1 You should be able to find many kinds of pretty paper at specialty stores.

2 For the cover, I bought a scrapbook and covered it with beautiful papers, but you can use any looseleaf binder or even medium-weight cardboard cut to size (with holes punched in it), decorated with papers, fabric, and/or trim.

3 On the cover, use a glitter pen or marker to write the name of the person who is receiving the scrapbook.

4 Use the grommet kit to reinforce the holes of the pages (and cover, if necessary) for the ribbon to go through.

---

potted grasses. I made a funny table skirt out of grass skirts that I keep in my little storage room and bring out once in a while for a luau or some other occasion. And I always have pieces of African cloth handy; here, to cover the table, I used two pieces of mud cloth. We served the buffet dinner in large, dark wooden platters and iron pots.

I decided to keep the menu simple to accommodate both children and adults, and to start with a snack that everybody would go for: homemade plantain chips and sweet potato chips. The meal picked up on the safari theme.

Putting together this menu, I thought beef short ribs would be the perfect entrée because they have such a chunky, primitive look. You can bake them, which makes preparing this meal very easy; I just brushed them with sauce to make them really flavorful and popped trays of them in the oven in a few batches. I added kale mashed potatoes (Dana likes anything thick and creamy), braised cabbage (her favorite), and a light salad. For dessert, I served perennial crowd—and kid—pleasers, sorbet and ice cream. What could be simpler?

With the invitation to the evening party, I had sent each guest a shoe box containing a blank page of pretty, handmade paper in one of Dana's favorite colors, punched with two holes, and craft supplies—glitter crayons, rubber stamps and a pad, note cards, and envelopes. I attached a note to the box asking that each person design a page for Dana—write out a quote, recall a memory, include a drawing or photograph. I explained that these pages would become part of a memory book, or what I call a book of inspiration. I prepared the front and back covers of the book and incorporated the guest list, menu, and recipes from the party.

After dinner, each person read from his or her page, after which I had them hand the paper to me. I passed ribbon through each page and tied the book closed, then presented it to Dana. This collaborative gift, like the entire day, was all about her and what makes her special.

Then it was time for drums and dancing. Dana's friends had created for her a symbolic dance of growth and renewal, drawing on percussive African and Brazilian rhythms. The performance symbolized the passing on of culture from one generation to the next. And it represented the rhythm of life. Rhythm binds us all together and confirms the energy in each of us. That was why I built the celebration around drums and dancing.

In creating Dana's rite of passage, I tried to find a way to combine storytelling, feasting, music, and gift-giving in a celebration that reflected who she is and what she's a part of. You might focus on similar elements if you plan to honor a young woman in your family with a rite-of-passage party. The main thing is to personalize the event. Find ways to incorporate your family's style, tastes, and history, and those of the child you are honoring.

The same is true if you want to give someone—or yourself—a rite of passage at any age. We never stop changing and growing, and for each of us there are certain times, all through the years, when we feel that our lives are about to change dramatically. It's exciting, and it's scary. The rite of passage is a way of celebrating the change among friends who'll help make a thread connecting your old life and your new life, with all its potential.

Dana's Rite-of-Passage Dinner for Sixteen

Plantain and Sweet Potato Chips

Citrus Green Salad with
Blue Cheese Vinaigrette

Oven-Barbecued Short Ribs of Beef

Spicy Braised Cabbage with Cashews

Kale Mashed Potatoes

Fruit sorbets and vanilla ice cream

Ginger ale

Coffee

Herbal tea

PLANTAIN AND SWEET POTATO CHIPS

Use a sharp knife, vegetable peeler, or a mandoline to make extra-thin slices.
SERVES 16

2½ pounds sweet potatoes, peeled and cut into ⅛-inch slices or as thinly as possible

2½ pounds medium-ripe plantains (6 to 8), peeled and cut into ⅛-inch slices or as thinly possible

Vegetable oil

Salt

In separate bowls of cold water, place the sweet potatoes and plantains for at least 1 hour after slicing. Drain the vegetables and pat them dry. In a deep fryer or deep heavy pot, heat ⅛ inch vegetable oil to 380 degrees. Fry vegetables separately in batches until golden brown. Do not overcrowd. Remove to paper towels. Salt lightly before serving.

CITRUS GREEN SALAD WITH BLUE CHEESE VINAIGRETTE

SERVES 16

½ cup lemon juice

4 teaspoons Dijon mustard

1 teaspoon salt

½ teaspoon ground white pepper

1½ cups extra virgin olive oil

1 cup crumbled blue cheese

16 to 20 cups torn romaine leaves

4 small navel oranges, peeled well and thinly sliced crosswise

1 small red onion, peeled, sliced, and separated into rings

In a small bowl, whisk together the lemon juice, mustard, salt, and white pepper. Slowly whisk in the olive oil until well blended. Stir in the blue cheese. Set aside.

In a large salad bowl, combine the romaine, orange slices, and onion rings. Pour the vinaigrette over the salad, toss, and serve immediately.

I kept the menu for Dana's dinner family-style with a sense of down-home comfort. Citrus Green Salad with Blue Cheese Vinaigrette, Oven-Barbecued Short Ribs of Beef, Spicy Braised Cabbage with Cashews, and Kale Mashed Potatoes—Dana's favorite.

OVEN-BARBECUED SHORT RIBS of BEEF

SERVES 16

4 large onions, peeled and sliced

4 large green bell peppers,
seeded and sliced

12 to 14 pounds beef short ribs

Salt and freshly ground black pepper
to taste

1½ cups hoisin sauce

1 cup flat beer

2 tablespoons cider vinegar

¼ cup grated fresh ginger

2 tablespoons brown sugar

2 tablespoons hot paprika

4 cloves garlic, minced

3 teaspoons dried oregano leaves

3 teaspoons dried thyme leaves

Preheat the broiler. In the bottom of a large pan or dutch oven, spread the sliced onions and peppers. Set aside.

Season the short ribs with salt and pepper. Working in batches, arrange the short ribs meaty side up on a rack in a broiler pan. Broil 4 to 5 minutes 4 to 5 inches from heat until well browned. Continue broiling, turning the ribs as necessary, until well browned on all sides. Transfer the ribs to a roasting pan.

Reduce the oven temperature to 350 degrees. In a bowl, whisk together the remaining ingredients. Pour half the barbecue sauce over the ribs. Tightly cover the roasting pan with aluminum foil, place in the oven, and braise for 2 hours.

Remove the foil, pour the remaining sauce over the beef and vegetables, and continue cooking uncovered ½ to 1 hour until the short ribs are very tender.

Transfer the short ribs and vegetables to a serving platter and keep warm. Skim the fat from the pan and pour the remaining sauce over the ribs to serve. The ribs may be made a day ahead, cooled, and refrigerated overnight. To serve, reheat in a covered pan in a warm oven.

SPICY BRAISED CABBAGE with CASHEWS

SERVES 16

4 tablespoons olive oil

4 tablespoons (½ stick) butter

2 large onions, peeled and sliced

4 pounds green cabbage, shredded

1 teaspoon crushed red pepper

2 teaspoons salt

1 teaspoon freshly ground black pepper

2 cups beef or chicken stock

1 cup chopped cashews

In a large pot, heat the oil and butter. Add the onions and sauté 4 to 5 minutes, until softened. Add the cabbage, crushed red pepper, salt, and black pepper. Stir until well combined. Add the stock and cook, covered, over medium heat 25 to 30 minutes. Stir in the chopped cashews.

KALE MASHED POTATOES

SERVES 16

6 pounds russet potatoes, peeled and cut into quarters

2 cloves garlic, peeled

1 cup (2 sticks) butter

4 teaspoons salt

2 teaspoons ground white pepper

1⅓ cups milk or heavy cream, heated until warm

Two 10-ounce packages frozen kale, cooked and squeezed dry

In a large pot with enough cold water to cover, place the potatoes and garlic. Bring to a boil and cook until tender, 15 to 20 minutes. Drain well in a colander and return the potatoes to the pot. Add the butter, salt, and white pepper, and mash with a potato masher. Continue mashing while gradually adding the warm milk. Stir in the kale and serve immediately.

APRIL

AN EASTER DINNER

I owe my love for ritual and celebration to my parents. They understood how family rituals help give each holiday its own distinctive, unforgettable flavor.

Even now, every time April comes around and the smell of spring hangs in the air, I'm taken back to my childhood in western Pennsylvania and my family's annual trek to Pittsburgh to buy us all new outfits for Easter. My three brothers got new suits—that didn't take long. Putting together *my* outfit was another matter. The first item to be chosen was, of course, my Easter bonnet. I come from a long line of hat-wearing ladies, and I like to continue the tradition not only in my own family but wherever else I can encourage it. (That's why at B. Smith's restaurant, Easter Sunday is also Hat Day. We ask our guests to display their creations proudly.)

This Easter I offered Roasted Leg of Lamb and (on table, from left) Orange-Zested Asparagus, Jalapeño-Honey-Glazed Ham with Steamed Okra and Roasted Red Bliss Potatoes, and Macaroni with Fontina and Gorgonzola Cheeses.

On those childhood pre-Easter shopping expeditions, it took me forever to pick one hat from among so many pretty ones. And once I'd chosen, there were other details to ponder. Which coat? Which dress? Which shoes? When I was finally decked out from head to toe, my mother went to look for her own bonnet.

But, as I suspect my parents knew, it wasn't only the fun of clothes shopping or the excitement of having something new that made this ritual so memorable; it was the way it felt, at Easter time, to shed those dark, heavy winter woolens and slip into something lightweight and light in color. My new outfit was like a brand-new beginning, a renewal. And that, of course, is what spring—and Easter and Easter eggs—is really all about. April is a time of blossoming (the name itself comes from the Latin word meaning "to open").

Today, when I prepare our home and table for Easter, I'm thinking about the light touch of tender new blossoms. I'm also thinking about my Aunt Nelly.

In our family, different people were responsible for hosting different major holidays. My mother was in charge of Thanksgiving, my grandma had Christmas, and the host and hostess for Easter were Uncle Roosevelt and Aunt Nelly. They lived in Clairton, Pennsylvania, about a half hour away. Even that short trip was an adventure to us, because our own town was so small that we considered little Clairton a city.

I remember walking into my aunt's house on Easter Sunday and immediately being enveloped in the wonderful aroma of food wafting out of the kitchen. The moment I walked in that door, I could smell homemade bread, lamb roasting in the oven, and ham baking—it wouldn't have been Easter without the big ham. All of these were served family-style to three generations sitting in great anticipation at the Easter table.

I was very fond of my Aunt Nelly, who was a warm and loving person, but she died when I was still a child. My uncle remarried and his new wife, Aunt Harriet, was the first woman I ever met who was an ordained minister. A handsome, impressive woman with a very commanding way, she took over Aunt Nelly's role as the person in charge of Easter dinners, and our annual Clairton visits continued without interruption.

Nowadays, I'm in charge of my own family's Easter, which means preparing the special meal, decorating the house, and making sure that everyone is properly

dressed. I've put my own mark on every aspect, borrowing from my childhood

My table is adorned with warm spring colors that help celebrate the season in full bloom.

memories but adapting what the women of my mother's generation did, so that what I serve will feel special to my family and guests, besides being a little less work for me.

My aunt always scored her ham, making diamond patterns all over it with a sharp knife until it resembled a pineapple, and then glazed it with brown sugar. The scoring made it easy to dot the ham with whole cloves, giving it a slightly spicy flavor and aroma. It also made this dish very decorative.

I too bake a ham for Easter (and roast a leg of lamb), scoring it and dotting it with cloves. But to save time, I buy a fully baked ham instead of a country ham.

MATERIALS

natural-colored basket

multipurpose or cold-water dye

water

rubber gloves

tub for dyeing (optional)

sponge brush (optional)

polyurethane sealer

1 Wash the basket with warm, soapy water to remove dust.

2 Select a dye color for the basket.

3 If you plan to immerse the basket in dye, select a container large enough. Dissolve the dye according to the package instructions. Wearing rubber gloves, sponge on the dye or immerse the basket in dyeing tub and let soak 20 minutes. Allow to dry thoroughly before applying a second coat. The color often dries brighter than you might expect, so don't redip until you see what color you've got.

4 Seal the color by applying a coat of polyurethane. Fill the basket with gardening items such as tools, seeds, a garden hat, a T-shirt, garden gloves, and children's books about flowers or gardening.

A great alternative to a traditional candy-filled Easter basket is a Garden Easter basket, filled with all the things kids need to start their very own garden.

And rather than using brown sugar to glaze it, I add a spicy jalapeño-honey glaze. With these two substantial dishes, all I need serve is some fresh, young spring vegetables: asparagus coated with orange-and-onion–flavored melted butter, new potatoes, and steamed okra (not technically a spring vegetable, but one of my favorites in any season).

This year, to please my stepdaughter, I also made one of *her* favorites—a creamy macaroni and cheese made with gorgonzola and fontina instead of American Cheddar. And I finished the meal by serving each guest a goblet of white chocolate tiramisú, a rich Italian dessert topped with raspberries and chocolate leaves.

Everybody feels special when you give each his own beautifully presented, individual dessert.

Easter for me will always be associated with my Aunt Nelly and her old-fashioned sense of how a table should be dressed, but at this time of year, I'm also drawn to the colors of crocuses and brand-new grass. So while my table is covered with a pale pink, auntlike cloth and decorated with pure white baskets and delicately painted eggs, I've chosen plates and napkins that remind me of the stronger pastels of spring flowers. If it weren't for my aunt, I might use a cool lavender or mint green tablecloth and dye or paint the baskets—but not in colors that shout. Spring is the cool calm before the fire of summer.

When I was a girl, my mother took charge of the baskets, and my brothers and I thought she was the finest basket decorator ever. What's more, we marveled at her talent for discovering secret spots where the Easter Bunny had hidden eggs that we kids had overlooked in our predinner hunt.

Nowadays, I give Easter baskets to the children in my extended family. This year, I thought it would be fun to make garden baskets. There's more than enough candy around at Easter time, and something new and different is always interesting to kids. I also believe it's important to give children things that help them learn: Gardening teaches them about nurturing living things, and about patience, too. In tending plants, children come to understand the cycles of the seasons and of birth, growth, death, and rebirth—which is what Easter and Easter eggs symbolize.

So rather than focus on chocolate eggs and marshmallow bunnies, I filled the baskets with tools and seeds and garden stakes, and tucked into each one a kids' gardening book and a small pot of herbs. I hoped that the plant, which was ready to be transplanted into the garden, would get the little ones started on their gardening project (and mobilize the adults to help them). Because children want instant gratification, I also decided to give them something they could enjoy right away. So, for each basket, I glued flower appliqués on a pair of new sneakers and a sweatshirt, and put flower stickers on a notebook to be used as a garden journal. Of course, there's nothing wrong with putting a few jelly beans and some chocolate in the Easter baskets, too. I'm not one to toss out the old traditions completely!

An Easter Dinner for Eight

Roasted Leg of Lamb

Jalapeño-Honey-Glazed Ham

Steamed Okra

Orange-Zested Asparagus

Roasted Red Bliss Potatoes

Macaroni with Fontina
and Gorgonzola Cheeses

Individual White Chocolate Tiramisù

Chardonnay, Silverado, Napa Valley, 1996
(or any other Chardonnay)

White zinfandel, Amador, Foothills, Amador County,
(or any other zinfandel)

ROASTED LEG OF LAMB

SERVES 8

6 to 8 pounds leg of lamb

⅓ cup peanut oil

4 cloves garlic, sliced

4 tablespoons chopped fresh rosemary
or 2 teaspoons dried rosemary leaves

Salt and freshly ground black pepper to
taste

Lamb Gravy (recipe follows)

Preheat the oven to 350 degrees. Have the meat at room temperature. In a small bowl, whisk the peanut oil, garlic, rosemary, salt, and pepper. On a rack in a shallow pan, place the lamb fat side up. Rub the lamb with the oil mixture. Roast, basting frequently, until the meat reaches medium doneness (a meat thermometer inserted in the thickest part of the meat will register 140–150 degrees), approximately 2 hours. Or roast the lamb to your desired degree of doneness. Slice and serve with Lamb Gravy.

LAMB GRAVY

YIELDS 2 CUPS

2 cups beef stock

⅓ cup Madeira wine

1 teaspoon cornstarch

1 tablespoon cold water

Salt and freshly ground black pepper
to taste

Remove the lamb from the roasting pan and drain the excess fat. Add the beef stock and Madeira to the pan. Bring to a boil, scraping up any browned bits from the bottom of the pan. Cook down until reduced by half. Meanwhile, in a small cup, mix the cornstarch and water until smooth. Whisk this into the beef stock mixture. Bring to a boil. Season with salt and pepper. Keep hot until ready to serve.

*Jalapeño-Honey-Glazed Ham with Steamed
Okra and Roasted Red Bliss Potatoes*

JALAPEÑO-HONEY-GLAZED HAM

When putting a large meal on the table, one way to simplify things is to prepare a fully cooked ham. This jalapeño glaze adds the just right amount of flavor.
SERVES 8

One 8- to 10-pound boneless smoked ham, cooked

½ cup honey

½ cup brown sugar

¼ cup bourbon

1 to 2 tablespoons minced fresh jalapeño pepper, or to taste

2 teaspoons dry mustard

1 teaspoon ground cloves

8 to 15 whole cloves

Heat the ham according to the package directions. Remove the ham from the oven 30 minutes before it is done. Score the outside of the ham with a sharp knife in a diamond pattern ¼ inch deep and about 1 inch apart. Combine the honey, brown sugar, bourbon, jalapeño pepper, dry mustard, and ground cloves. Mix well and brush over the outside of the ham. Stick a whole clove in the center of each diamond. Continue baking the ham for 30 minutes, basting frequently. Let the ham stand at room temperature 10 to 15 minutes before slicing.

STEAMED OKRA

SERVES 8

2 pounds medium okra pods

2 tablespoons butter

1 teaspoon salt

Rinse the okra thoroughly in cold water. Place into a steaming basket over 1 to 2 inches of boiling water. Cover and cook until tender but crisp, about 5 minutes. Toss with the butter and salt. Serve warm.

ORANGE-ZESTED ASPARAGUS

SERVES 8

6 cups water
1 teaspoon salt
2 pounds asparagus (bottom inch cut off)
3 tablespoons butter
½ cup orange juice
4 tablespoons orange zest strips
1 orange, peeled and thinly sliced
1 medium red onion, sliced
Salt and freshly ground black pepper to taste

In a large deep skillet, bring the water and salt to a boil. You will need to work in batches. Place some of the asparagus gently in the skillet. Boil 5 to 6 minutes, until the spears are tender. Remove with tongs. Repeat until all the asparagus are cooked. Drain the skillet. Over medium heat, add the butter, orange juice, and zest. Cook until the butter is melted. Pour over the asparagus. Add the orange slices, red onion, salt, and pepper.

ROASTED RED BLISS POTATOES

SERVES 8

8 cups small Red Bliss potatoes, unpeeled, scrubbed, and cut in half
½ cup olive oil
1 teaspoon salt
1 teaspoon freshly ground black pepper

Preheat the oven to 350 degrees.

In a large roasting pan, combine all the ingredients and toss thoroughly to coat the potatoes with the seasonings. Roast the potatoes 50 to 60 minutes, until they are golden and crisp. Serve immediately.

MACARONI WITH FONTINA AND GORGONZOLA CHEESES

SERVES 8

Salt

1 pound uncooked elbow macaroni

¼ pound fontina cheese

¼ pound Gorgonzola cheese

2 tablespoons butter

½ cup half-and-half

Freshly ground black pepper to taste

Chopped chives or parsley to garnish

In a medium pot, bring 4 quarts of water to a boil. Add a pinch of salt and the macaroni. Cook until tender, about 8 to 10 minutes. In a colander, drain the macaroni and return it to the pot. Fold in the cheese, butter, and half-and-half. Season with the pepper. Serve in a heated bowl and garnish with chopped chives or chopped parsley.

INDIVIDUAL WHITE CHOCOLATE TIRAMISÚS

These individual tiramisús look super-elegant served in large stemmed wine goblets— but you could also use individual serving bowls, as long as they're deep enough.
SERVES 8

WHITE CHOCOLATE CREAM

½ cup milk

4 ounces good-quality white chocolate, broken into pieces

¼ cup sugar

8 ounces mascarpone

¾ cup heavy cream

1 teaspoon vanilla extract

¼ cup raspberry liqueur (crème de cassis) or raspberry-flavored syrup

4 tablespoons grated bittersweet or semisweet chocolate

16 very thin slices sponge or angel food cake

12 whole strawberries

(continued)

To make the white chocolate cream, heat the milk over low-medium heat until bubbles form around the edge of the saucepan. Place the white chocolate pieces in a small bowl and pour the hot milk over. Whisk until the chocolate is completely melted. Cool to room temperature.

Meanwhile, in a medium bowl, whisk the sugar into the mascarpone. Set aside. In a small, chilled bowl, whip the cream with the vanilla until soft peaks form (do not overbeat). Whisk the white chocolate mixture into the mascarpone. Fold in the whipped cream. The texture should be like lightly whipped cream; if it doesn't "flow," thin the mixture slightly by stirring in some milk, 1 tablespoon at a time.

Spoon the liqueur evenly over the cake slices. Place one slice of cake in the bottom of each goblet. Spoon half of the cream mixture over the cake slices (about 2½ tablespoons for each slice). Sprinkle each with ½ tablespoon of the grated chocolate. Slice 8 strawberries and place some slices over the chocolate in each goblet. Repeat the cake, cream, and chocolate layers. Refrigerate for 4 to 8 hours.

To make the chocolate leaves, line a plate with waxed paper. In a double boiler over low heat, melt the grated semisweet chocolate. Remove the chocolate from the heat. Using a pastry brush, spread the underside of each leaf with a layer of chocolate. Place the painted leaves, chocolate side up, on the prepared plate. Freeze until the chocolate is set. Carefully peel the leaf off the chocolate, handling the chocolate leaf as little as possible. Return the leaves to the freezer if the chocolate is melting.

Just before serving, top each tiramisú with raspberries and garnish each with a strawberry half and chocolate leaves.

NOTE: To make the tiramisús a day ahead, leave out the strawberry slices in between the layers. Sprinkle the raspberries over the top just before serving.

A Spring Hooky Day Luncheon

By the time spring comes around, I'm starting to feel just a little restless. And, I'm also feeling the need to catch up with good friends whom I haven't seen for far too long. All winter, we've hunkered down and taken care of business without putting aside time for pure fun—the kind of fun you have when you get together with a bunch of girlfriends and talk about men.

A woman I know who wanted to reconnect with her friends hired a mini-van and driver to take them off on an all-day shopping spree. She treated them to lunch, and on the return trip gave out prizes for the best bargains found! At the beginning of the day, everyone felt a little guilty about taking time off from work. But by afternoon, they all admitted feeling revived and refreshed after just a short respite from the daily grind.

Inspired by this story, I decided to call my own friends and coax them into taking a day off and joining me for a Spring Hooky Day celebration. My idea of a truly great day—and I suspected it would be theirs too—was to have no plans at all. It would be pure luxury for us to just slip out of our shoes, forget about makeup, and kick back: Sip some wine, catch up on gossip, and get totally silly.

My challenge was to come up with a meal that would be flavorful and interesting, but practically no work at all. The solution was a light but tasty entrée based on a traditional recipe from the Baule people—Kedjenou chicken, which is steamed in a clay pot. All you have to do is put the chicken into an ovenproof 6–8-quart lidded casserole along with some vegetables and herbs, cover it, put it in the oven, and wait, shaking it occasionally so the food doesn't stick (in fact, in the Baule language, *Kedjenou* means "to shake"). While the ingredients steam themselves, their flavors meld into something truly delicious. This simple, meal-in-a-pot technique is used in cuisines around the world: The Moroccans make tangines, the Germans have romertopfs, in Provence they cook tians, and we Americans borrowed casseroles from the French.

The secret of a good Kedjenou chicken lies in the pot itself. You can use anything heavy and deep enough to hold all the ingredients, with a tight-fitting lid to keep the steam in. I happen to have an authentic Baule pot, made for this purpose, that I bought at the Museum for African Art in New York City. Baule women have passed down their pottery art through the generations. The pot I bought came from a women's cooperative in the central plains of the Ivory Coast.

The Baule make their pots out of clay dug from the banks of streams or from pits in the earth. They bake each one over an open fire of straw or wood, then blacken it on smoldering sawdust and, while it's still hot, brush it with a liquid made from leaves and tree bark, all of which gives a beautiful, dark, metallic look to the finished product. Different styles of pottery are used for different purposes— some for storing liquids used in rituals, others to carry water and palm wine, and others still for cooking. The chicken in the recipe that follows is prepared in a round-bottomed pot with a narrow neck that's sealed shut during the cooking.

I wanted the table setting to reflect the earthy beauty of the pottery and the simplicity of the menu (chicken, vegetables, curried rice, and a fresh-pineapple dessert). So I used an oatmeal-textured cloth and a set of handsome brown pottery plates—also from the museum. Then I put out place cards for each of my guests. Even when you're not entertaining a large number of people, it's fun to have place cards, and personalizing things makes everybody feel special.

My hooky-playing guests enjoyed lunch, and "doing nothing" turned out to be a highly successful party theme. In fact, we're making it an annual ritual. I highly recommend you throw a Spring Hooky Day party of your own. Most people can take a personal day off, and there's a kind of guilty pleasure in partying when everyone else is working. Especially on one of those glorious days when everyone has spring fever, a Hooky Day party is just the tonic we all need.

A Hooky Day celebration is something you can enjoy with your children, too. I shouldn't be encouraging it, but I have wonderful memories of the times my mother would announce a "personal day" and let me skip school so we could do something together that she considered worthwhile, like a trip to the museum or even the circus. Playing hooky with your kids is a sure way to deepen your bonds; after all, you're being naughty together, locked in a conspiracy against the rest of the grown-up world. That's an experience a child is likely to remember for years to come.

A Spring Hooky Day
Luncheon for Six

Kedjenou Chicken

Curried Rice

Fresh Pineapple
and Coconut
Sorbet with
Rum-Spiked Syrup

Minted iced tea

Chardonnay, Kendall-Jackson
Vintner's Reserve, 1997
(or any other Chardonnay)

*Kedjenou Chicken
with Curried Rice*

KEDJENOU CHICKEN

SERVES 6

1 habanero pepper

½ cup hot rich chicken stock

⅛ teaspoon dried saffron

One 28-ounce can whole plum tomatoes, sliced, or 3 fresh tomatoes, sliced

3 onions, chopped

4 cloves garlic, minced

3 medium carrots

1 large yellow bell pepper, cut into strips

1 cup diced celery

3 bay leaves

1½ teaspoons dried thyme leaves

5½–6 pounds frying chickens cut into serving pieces, skin removed

Salt and freshly ground black pepper to taste

One 10-ounce package thawed frozen tiny peas or 1½ cups fresh peas, blanched

½ cup chopped fresh parsley

Curried Rice (recipe follows)

Preheat the oven to 350 degrees. Place the habanero pepper in the chicken stock for 20 minutes. Remove the softened habanero pepper, cut away the stem, and seed. Dice and return to the stock. Add the saffron to the stock.

In the bottom of a large, heavy pot, arrange the tomatoes. Layer the remaining vegetables (except for the peas and parsley), stock, and chicken on top. Add salt and pepper. Cover the pot tightly with aluminum foil. Place in the oven and bake 90 minutes. Remove the pot and shake occasionally while baking. Pour into a wide-rimmed bowl. Scatter the peas over the top and sprinkle with parsley. Serve with Curried Rice.

CURRIED RICE

SERVES 6

1¾ cups water

¾ teaspoon salt

2 cups apple juice

1½ cups uncooked white rice

2 tablespoons butter

1 large onion, minced

2 cloves garlic, minced

1 tablespoon curry powder

In a large saucepan, combine the water, salt, apple juice, and rice. Bring to a boil, cover, reduce heat, and simmer 15 minutes or until the liquid is absorbed. In a large skillet, melt the butter. Add the onion and garlic, and cook until soft. Stir in the curry powder. Add the rice, stirring until heated through and evenly coated with curry. Serve hot.

FRESH PINEAPPLE AND COCONUT SORBET WITH RUM-SPIKED SYRUP

SERVES 6

1 fresh pineapple, peeled, sliced, and cored

1 cup pineapple juice

Spiced Sugar Syrup (recipe follows)

4 tablespoons dark rum

6 scoops coconut sorbet

Shredded fresh or sweetened shredded coconut for garnish

Arrange the sliced pineapple on a serving plate. In a saucepan, heat the pineapple juice. Add the Spiced Sugar Syrup and rum. Bring to a boil. Reduce the heat. Simmer until the sauce thickens slightly. Cool to room temperature. Pour the sauce over the pineapple. Refrigerate. Right before serving, place a scoop of coconut sorbet in the center of each pineapple ring. Garnish with coconut before serving.

SPICED SUGAR SYRUP

YIELDS 1/4 CUP

1 cup sugar

2 cups water

1 cinnamon stick

3 tablespoons sliced fresh ginger

4 whole cloves

1 teaspoon ground ginger

In a saucepan, simmer all of the ingredients about 10 minutes. Strain ingredients through a fine sieve. Cool to room temperature and refrigerate, covered, until ready to use.

MAY

A Mother's Day Celebration for Mothers and Others

There's no day quite like the one we set aside to honor our mothers. No other holiday has that same mix of tribute and warmth, and few occasions make us so eager to do everything properly—the way Mom would want it done. After all, what better way to honor your mother than to show her how well she's raised you!

A mom deserves special attention every day. All the more reason, on Mother's Day, to put her on a pedestal and give her extraspecial treatment. She should be showered with flowers and gifts and whisked off to a restaurant or, if she prefers, honored with a favorite meal that's been lovingly prepared at home (by someone other than her!).

Creating a special meal at home is a wonderful way to honor someone, whether it's your mother or a mother figure. Many people are afraid to cook something special for their mothers because they don't think they can measure up to her standards. But it doesn't have

While my real mother has passed on, Mother's Day is a day to say thank you to anyone who is a role model in our lives. In this case Clarice Taylor is mine, and I thank her with all my heart.

to be complicated. It's just a matter of paying attention to those little things that make an occasion of a simple meal. At B. Smith's, I see grown sons and daughters going to no end of trouble to make just the right arrangements for this day, down to the last detail—a limo to pick Mom up and deliver her to the restaurant. Treating your mother to a memorable day in your home isn't all that different.

My own mother is no longer with me, but she left me an incredible legacy by being such a wonderful homemaker. She gardened, she preserved, she was a decorator, she painted, she restored furniture, and most especially, she set a great table. Preparing a special meal was a joy to her, not an obligation, and she happily passed this passion on to me.

Oddly enough, I realized only recently that I've dedicated myself to being a hostess and a professional restaurateur because of my mother. By teaching me her recipes and entertaining style and by developing in me a sense of how to pay attention to your guests, my mother not only shaped my lifestyle and made me who I am, but also helped me find a career. When I wake up on Mother's Day— or any other day of the year, for that matter—I think of her and thank her for all she gave me.

In honor of her, I make a Mother's Day luncheon every year. Although she can't be with me—neither can my stepdaughter, Dana, on this day—I still like to keep the celebration going, but I've expanded the traditional definition of "mother." In today's world, there are many different ways to nurture; you don't have to have given birth to be a mother to someone. So I give a grownups-only "Mothers and Others" luncheon on Mother's Day for myself and other traditional and nontraditional "moms."

My guest list might include people who've mentored me, and others for whom I fill that role. This year, I invited a lady who, when my mother died, told me she was now going to be a mom to me. Some of my guests can't be with their kids or their mothers, and still others have never been parents but are great nurturers. A friend of mine who's a single dad told me his children send him Father's Day *and* Mother's Day cards because he's both a mom and dad to them. So now I include single fathers on my Mother's Day list. And I honor all my guests with a meal that my mother would have wholeheartedly approved of.

Whether you're entertaining your own mother for lunch or honoring her in her absence, you'll be more likely to do a great job if you plan something that's simple to prepare, but also very flavorful. For my entrée, I made a chicken breast with a seasoned rock shrimp sauce; the sauce gives the chicken special flair. I added brown rice to the couscous pilaf for flavor and an extra layer of texture. And even the sherry vinaigrette dressing on the salad of baby spinach, which is influenced by New Orleans cuisine, has a little Creole seasoning in it.

When I think of my mother, I think of someone who was always very ladylike, so I want the meal I prepare for Mother's Day to be pretty. In this menu, baby asparagus (or, if you can find them, fiddlehead ferns) did the trick, and the vegetables in the pale yellow couscous added a touch of extra color. My mother would always have a beautiful cake or pie sitting on the side—when you sat down at the table, you could see that the meal was going to end on a high note. The orange-mango layer cake I made looked beautiful, and gave a special twist to the idea of something sweet.

If I were treating my mother, everything would have to be done just right—or she'd let me know! So my Mother's Day luncheon is about the right combinations of foods, the right colors, the right china and flatware—a little up to date, but still delicate and proper—and, of course, the right flowers. A classic floral arrangement says "May" and "Mother."

To me, that's what Mother's Day is all about. You don't have to celebrate it, but why not? When you cook a meal and make everything look pretty, it makes people feel good. At my luncheon, I wanted to honor my guests in the same way that I would have honored my own mother—so that they would feel special, and she would look down on this party and say, "You did good."

A Mother's Day Luncheon for Four

Salad of Baby Spinach
and Radicchio with Sherry Vinaigrette
—

Creole Chicken with Rock Shrimp Sauce
—

Sautéed Baby Asparagus
—

Couscous Rice Pilaf
—

Orange-Mango Triple Sec Layer Cake
—

Pinot Grigio, Flora Springs, Napa Valley, 1997
(or any other Pinot Grigio)

SALAD OF BABY SPINACH AND RADICCHIO WITH SHERRY VINAIGRETTE

SERVES 4

⅔ cup walnut oil

⅓ cup sherry vinegar

½ teaspoon Creole seasoning

6 cups lightly packed baby spinach, washed

6 radicchio leaves, cut into julienne strips

In a small bowl, mix the walnut oil, sherry vinegar, and Creole seasoning.

In a large bowl, toss together the spinach and radicchio with just enough vinaigrette to coat lightly. Serve. (You'll have extra vinaigrette to use later in the week.)

CREOLE CHICKEN WITH ROCK SHRIMP SAUCE

The cuisine at B. Smith's restaurant at Union Station in D.C. is a combination of Cajun, Creole, and Southern. It influenced me to create this dish. Try it with rock shrimp or crawfish. They both give the sauce a special flair. **SERVES 4**

1 tablespoon vegetable oil

4 whole skinless and boneless chicken breasts

Salt and freshly ground black pepper to taste

1 tablespoon butter

¼ cup chopped onion

1 tablespoon minced garlic

2 tablespoons seeded, finely chopped green bell pepper

2 tablespoons seeded, finely chopped red bell pepper

2 tablespoons all-purpose flour

¾ cup dry white wine

⅛ teaspoon cayenne pepper, or to taste

(continued)

In a 12-inch nonstick sauté pan over high heat, heat the oil. Add the chicken and sprinkle with salt and pepper. Cover. Brown the chicken pieces on both sides, about 5 minutes per side. Transfer the chicken to a platter.

In the sauté pan over medium heat, melt the butter. Add the onion, garlic, and bell peppers, and sauté for 2 minutes. Stir in the flour; cook 30 seconds longer, stirring constantly. Add the white wine, scraping any brown bits from the bottom of the pan. Add the cayenne pepper, Creole seasoning, bay leaves, chicken stock,

Creole Chicken with Rock Shrimp Sauce,
Sautéed Baby Asparagus, and Couscous Rice Pilaf

1 teaspoon Creole seasoning

2 bay leaves

¾ cup chicken stock

½ cup peeled, seeded, chopped fresh or
canned Italian plum tomatoes

1 pound rock shrimp or crawfish meat

1 tablespoon finely chopped fresh parsley
for garnish

tomatoes, and chicken. Bring the sauce to a boil; cover. Reduce the heat and simmer 10 minutes, or until the chicken pieces are cooked through and tender.

Add the rock shrimp; cover. Cook 5 minutes longer, stirring occasionally. Remove the bay leaves. Divide the chicken among four plates and pour equal amounts of sauce on top. Garnish with the parsley. Serve.

COUSCOUS RICE PILAF

SERVES 4

1 tablespoon butter or olive oil

½ cup diced carrots

2 cloves garlic, minced

2 cups boiling chicken stock or water

1 cup uncooked instant long-grain
brown rice

½ teaspoon salt (optional)

¾ cup uncooked couscous

2 scallions, cut into ¼-inch thick slices
on the diagonal

In a medium saucepan, over medium heat, melt the butter. Add the carrots and garlic. Sauté 3 minutes, stirring occasionally.

Add the stock. Stir in the brown rice and salt; cover. Lower heat; simmer 5 minutes. Stir in the couscous and scallions; cover and cook 1 minute. Remove from the heat and let sit 5 minutes. Transfer to a serving bowl, stirring to fluff up. Serve.

SAUTÉED BABY ASPARAGUS

As a side dish, baby or regular asparagus works fine here; but if you are lucky enough to find fiddlehead ferns, they would be a delicious replacement.   **SERVES 4**

1 tablespoon butter
1 pound baby asparagus
Salt and freshly ground black pepper
to taste

In a skillet large enough to hold the asparagus in a single layer, melt the butter. Add the asparagus. Cover and cook over low heat about 4 minutes, or until tender-crisp. Sprinkle with salt and pepper. Serve.

This year's Mother's Day bouquet features roses, tulips, and lilacs.

ORANGE-MANGO TRIPLE SEC LAYER CAKE

SERVES 12

CAKE

3 cups cake flour

2½ teaspoons baking powder

½ teaspoon baking soda

¼ teaspoon salt

8 large egg whites

1¾ cups granulated sugar, divided

1 cup (2 sticks) butter, softened

1 teaspoon orange extract

1 teaspoon grated orange zest

1 cup buttermilk

SYRUP

3 tablespoons orange juice

3 tablespoons granulated sugar

3 tablespoons triple sec

FILLING

¾ cup granulated sugar

¼ cup cornstarch

⅛ teaspoon salt

1¼ cups fresh-squeezed orange juice

2 large egg yolks

¼ cup fresh-squeezed lemon juice

4 tablespoons butter

2 teaspoons grated orange zest

FROSTING

1 box (16 ounces) powdered sugar

½ cup (1 stick) butter, softened

1½ teaspoons grated orange peel

6 to 8 tablespoons heavy cream

Red and yellow food coloring (optional)

2 mangoes, peeled

Strawberries or raspberries for garnish

To make the cake, preheat the oven to 350 degrees. Grease three 9-inch round cake pans. Line the bottoms with waxed paper. Grease the waxed paper liners and dust with flour; tap out excess.

Into a medium bowl, sift the flour, baking powder, baking soda, and salt. Set aside. In the large bowl of an electric mixer, on medium speed, beat the egg whites until they are the texture of softly whipped cream. Gradually beat in ¼ cup of the sugar; beat just until stiff peaks form. Set aside.

In another large bowl, with the mixer on medium speed, beat the butter until creamy. Gradually beat in the remaining 1½ cups sugar. Beat 2 minutes until fluffy. Beat in the orange extract and orange zest. With the mixer on low speed, alternately beat in the flour mixture and the buttermilk, ending with the flour mixture, beating just until blended. Stir in a spoonful of beaten egg whites. Gently fold in the remaining egg whites, one third at a time, just until blended. Divide the batter evenly among the cake pans. Bake 25 to 30 minutes, or until a toothpick inserted in the center comes out clean. Let the cakes cool in the pans 10 minutes. Run a knife around the sides of the pans and turn the cakes out onto racks. Let cool completely.

To make the syrup, in a small saucepan, combine the orange juice and sugar. Bring to a boil; boil 1 minute. Stir in the triple sec. Let cool.

To make the filling, in a medium saucepan, whisk the sugar, cornstarch, and salt. Add the orange juice and whisk until smooth. Cook over medium heat, stirring constantly, until the mixture comes to a boil. Boil 1 minute, stirring frequently. Remove the pan from the heat. In a small bowl, whisk the egg yolks and lemon juice together. Gradually whisk in half of the hot orange juice mixture. Gradually stir the yolk mixture back into the saucepan. Return the pan to the heat. Stir until the filling comes to a simmer; simmer 1 minute. Remove the pan from the heat. Add the butter and orange zest; stir until the butter melts. Pour the filling into a clean small bowl. Let cool. Cover and refrigerate until cold, about 4 hours.

To make the frosting, in a large bowl, combine the powdered sugar, butter, orange peel, and 6 tablespoons of the cream. With an electric mixer, on medium-low speed, beat until blended. With the mixer on medium-high speed, beat until the frosting is smooth and fluffy, adding the remaining cream as necessary for the proper consistency. If desired, add enough food coloring to make the frosting pale orange; beat until blended.

To assemble the cake, set aside ⅓ cup of the orange filling for the top of the cake. Chop enough mango to equal 1 cup. Thinly slice the remaining mango. Place one cake layer on a serving plate and brush with one third of the syrup. Spread with half of the remaining orange filling. Evenly spoon on ½ cup of the chopped mango. Top with the second cake layer and brush again with one third of the syrup, topping with the remaining half of the orange filling. Top with the last cake layer and brush with the remaining third of the syrup. Spread the frosting over the sides and in a 1-inch border on top of the cake. Spoon the reserved ⅓ cup orange filling inside the frosting border and spread to smooth over. Arrange the mango slices and strawberries or raspberries on top as garnish. Serve immediately or refrigerate until serving.

A Memorial Day Barbecue

Ever since I was a child, I've considered Memorial Day to be the beginning of summer—even though summer doesn't officially start for another month. It's the beginning of the barbecue season, the beginning of the summer-house season, and, along with that, the beginning of houseguest season.

Back in my childhood, the last weekend in May meant that school vacation was right around the corner. Even now, I'm filled with anticipation as this long weekend draws near, because it marks the start of Long Island's summer invasion. After a long winter hibernation, B. Smith's restaurant in Sag Harbor throws open its doors and the whole town comes to life again. For New Yorkers, Sag Harbor and the surrounding communities—known as the Hamptons—has become the summer retreat of choice; it offers the best of Manhattan—the eateries and bars, the gourmet grocery stores and galleries—transplanted to an exquisite seaside location.

On Memorial Day, home owners and renters start to make their first trips to town to get their places ready for the summer. Passing through the quiet side streets, you can see signs of activity that let us know the summer community is coming back to life. Bags of groceries and other essentials are being unpacked from cars. Shutters are being painted. Ladies with garden gloves are planting baby geraniums in their window boxes. And intrepid souls are shivering around outdoor grills, waiting for the first hot dogs of the season. So what if the weather is a little chilly? They're happy to be back outdoors.

I like grilling all year round—I don't mind putting on my hood and boots and braving the elements. But most

When May rolls around, Dan and I kick off summer by breaking out the grill—something we wait for all year long.

people save their first barbecue for Memorial Day, which is why my Memorial Day menu is centered around buffalo steaks. (You could use ordinary steak, but why not go for something a little different?) Steaks are a great basis for outdoor entertaining, especially when you've got plenty of other things to take care of—whether it's a restaurant to open, a house to prepare, or friends to visit with. You can't cook anything quicker than a steak, and unless you overcook it, you can't damage it. And I know that if the weather doesn't cooperate with my barbecue plans I could use a grill pan and cook the same thing inside on top of the stove. (At this time of year in the Northeast, you never know from hour to hour if it's going to be balmy, chilly, or raining.)

I believe that entertaining well takes not only flair and imagination, a willingness to experiment with new ideas, and a desire to make your guests feel special; you also have to be very practical. There's no point in planning an exquisite meal with a brand-new twist and designing the most inventive table setting if you're not going to be able to pull it off.

I designed my whole Memorial Day menu to be flexible for inside or outside cooking and dining; summery, yet warming at the same time; and simple to prepare but a little unusual, so it would be interesting and fun for my guests and easy on me. One of the things I like best about Memorial Day is that we get to visit with people whom we've barely seen all winter. It's a very social occasion, and I wanted to serve a meal we could sit and socialize over.

Along with the buffalo steaks, the lentil salad is different, as well as hearty—and it's a dish you can prepare ahead of time. I always want to serve tomatoes in celebration of summer; but I have to deal with the fact that it's still too early in the season for the sweet, vine-ripened local variety. So I roast and layer my tomatoes with grilled sweet Vidalia onions, which are easy to find this time of the year. When you cook a tomato, it brings out the sweetness in it; and the layering makes for a nice presentation.

Creating an attractive table setting for this meal is relatively simple: the garden provides a perfect backdrop, and bowls of brightly colored vegetables, along with my potted herbs, supply all the decoration and color I need to make this occasion feel like true summer.

But it's only May, and as the day grows late, a chill creeps into the air. So, after the main course, we all wander inside and sit down to chat over a tray of assorted cheeses and a glass of port. I've always considered cheese to be very comforting as a dessert course, especially with a little port. When you bring out a cheese tray, it means that you plan to hang out after dinner and relax. When I'm planning this type of dessert course, I like to select three or four cheeses—soft, semisoft, and hard—for a variety of tastes, textures, and flavors. (You could serve a soft chèvre; a camembert or brie, which have soft, edible crusts; a Maytag blue, Danish Stilton, or Gorgonzola; and a Cheddar, Gruyère, or Parmigiano-Reggiano.) Cheese should always be served at room temperature. Along with the cheeses, I like to serve fresh, ripe fruits such as grapes, strawberries, and figs, as well as nuts and crackers or French bread.

A Memorial Day Barbecue for Six

Rosemary-Marinated Buffalo Steaks

Oven-Roasted Tomatoes
with Grilled Vidalia Onions

Lively Lentil Salad

Assorted cheese and fruit dessert tray

Zinfandel, Ravenswood, Alexander Valley, 1997
(or any other zinfandel)

Taylor Fladgate Tawny 10-Year Port
(or any other port)

*Rosemary-Marinated Buffalo Steaks,
Oven-Roasted Tomatoes with Grilled Vidalia
Onions, and Lively Lentil Salad*

ROSEMARY-MARINATED BUFFALO STEAKS

I often use buffalo steaks because they are lower in cholesterol and fat than beef or chicken. The lemon tenderizes the meat and the rosemary infuses a great flavor.

SERVES 6

¾ cup olive oil

3 tablespoons fresh-squeezed lemon juice

Freshly ground black pepper to taste

Leaves of several sprigs of fresh rosemary, chopped

6 medium buffalo steaks

To prepare the marinade, combine all ingredients but the meat in a small glass bowl. Pour the marinade over the steaks, coating both sides. You can cook the steaks immediately or refrigerate them; remove them from the refrigerator about 30 minutes before grilling so that they will be at room temperature when you place them on the grill. Once the steaks are on the grill, watch them carefully. Generally speaking, it is best to turn them only once. Cooking time varies with different grills. A 1-inch-thick steak will take approximately 6 to 7 minutes on each side to cook to medium-rare. I prefer my buffalo steaks rare and soft to the touch. You might want to refer to your grill manual for specific instructions on how to cook your steaks to your taste.

OVEN-ROASTED TOMATOES WITH GRILLED VIDALIA ONIONS

SERVES 6

6 medium tomatoes, halved

2 large Vidalia onions, peeled and thinly sliced

Herb-infused olive oil

Salt and freshly ground black pepper to taste

Chopped chives for garnish

Broil the tomatoes, close to a medium heat, until slightly softened, about 3 to 4 minutes. Skewer large slices of onion, brush with olive oil, and grill on both sides until slightly soft, about 3 to 4 minutes on each side. Remove the skewer. Arrange an onion slice between each of the six tomato halves. Drizzle with the herb-infused olive oil and sprinkle with salt, pepper, and chives. Serve warm or at room temperature.

NOTE: The tomatoes can be broiled in advance to save time.

LIVELY LENTIL SALAD

SERVES 6

1 cup French green lentils

4 cups water

2 bay leaves

2½ teaspoons chopped fresh thyme or 1½ teaspoons dried thyme leaves

1 clove garlic, minced

½ cup minced red onion

¾ cup diced celery

¾ cup diced green, red, or yellow bell pepper

1 teaspoon ground cumin

1 teaspoon chopped fresh oregano

2 tablespoons chopped fresh parsley

½ cup extra virgin olive oil

3 tablespoons red wine vinegar

Salt and freshly ground black pepper to taste

4 cups salad greens

Tomato wedges for garnish

Rinse the lentils. In a medium saucepan, bring the water, lentils, bay leaves, and 1½ teaspoons of the fresh thyme (1 teaspoon if dried) to a boil. Reduce the heat and simmer 20 to 25 minutes, until tender not mushy, stirring occasionally. In a large bowl, combine the next seven ingredients. In a separate bowl, whisk the oil and vinegar together. Drain the lentils and discard the bay leaves. Toss the lentils with the vegetables. Add the oil-and-vinegar mixture. Add the remaining thyme and season to taste with salt and pepper. Serve warm on a bed of salad greens. Garnish with tomato wedges.

WEEKENDER GIFT BASKETS

On Memorial Day weekend, the Hampton Jitney bus service and the Long Island Rail Road switch to their summer schedules to accommodate the hordes of vacationers and their armies of guests. People do a lot of entertaining in the Hamptons, and our house is no exception. I enjoy being able to invite people to my place after having spent years being a "weekender" myself, staying at hotels and motels near the shore or enjoying the hospitality of friends. Back in those days, while my hosts planned ways to entertain and feed me and their other guests, I had fun planning house gifts.

Finding a great gift for your host and hostess can be a challenge, but it needn't be a chore. Houseguesting weekends tend to revolve around eating, so you're always safe bringing some kind of special food. Although I'm involved with food all the time, I'm always happy to be given something I might not treat myself to: a small box of spectacular chocolates, for example, or something home-made (by my guest or by the person who sold it to them). And I love it when a friend who's a connoisseur of something like cheese or wine brings a favorite for me to taste.

Gifts don't have to be expensive, but they should be thoughtful. Unless you know it's something your host will especially enjoy, don't fall back on that old standby—the bottle of wine. Instead, start with a theme that fits your host's taste and lifestyle, and use that as the basis for a basket of gifts. If you pick an assortment of items, you can be pretty sure that one or another of them will please someone in the host family. Be adventurous; look for items that have unusual labels or come in interesting jars. The packaging can be as much fun as what's inside.

Here are a few ideas to get you thinking. They're ideal "summer's coming" gifts for the home. If you use your imagination, you're sure to come up with some great ideas of your own.

- a variety of unusual beers from all around the world

- a selection of dried pastas and distinctive pasta sauces from the gourmet grocery

- different kinds of aromatic wood for the barbecue, such as hickory, oak, mesquite, and fruit woods

- a group of interesting oils and vinegars, condiments, or barbecue sauces

- a selection of cocktail items such as smoked oysters, olives, pâté, crackers, dips, nuts

- a variety of liqueurs that can be used as drinks or in great last-minute sauces for poached or fresh fruits

- a sundae kit with various toppings— nuts, maraschino cherries, chocolate and rainbow sprinkles, etc.

- fruit-flavored teas, which make for delicious iced teas—add a pretty glass pitcher as well

- a variety of jellies, jams, and marmalades that can be used as toppings on bread or desserts, or in cooking

- a selection of herb- and fruit-flavored butters

- unusual seeds and/or bulbs and pretty garden gloves

- a pet lover's basket filled with a pet brush, chew toy, leash or collar, food and water bowls, place mat, and treats

- a variety of gifts for the person or couple who entertain: bottle opener, ashtray, pilsner glasses, deck of cards, poker chips, and coasters

- a baby bundle for hosts with a newborn that includes a stuffed animal, a changing mat, soaps, lotions, powders, cotton balls and swabs, and a rubber duck

The best gift—big or small, funny or serious—is always the one that's specially tailored to the person receiving it. It's a gift you wouldn't give to anyone else. Is your host an avid gardener? Is there a new baby in the family? Is this a crossword puzzle fanatic? A baseball fan? An art-loving couple? Once you've found the perfect theme, look for a container that's amusing and unique. It could be a tray, a basket, or a flea market find; it could even be part of the gift itself. Half the trick of giving a great house gift lies in the presentation.

JUNE

A JUNETEENTH CELEBRATION

June 19, 1865, was a day of great jubilation that we commemorate by observing Juneteenth. It's a fun and festive celebration, but there's a serious piece of history behind it: Juneteenth memorializes the end of slavery—the *real* end. Although President Lincoln issued the Emancipation Proclamation on January 1, 1863, freedom took a long time coming, especially in places such as Arkansas and Texas. It wasn't until mid-1865 that General Gordon Granger arrived in Galveston with federal troops to free the slaves of Texas.

Why it took two years, six months, and nineteen days for the people of Texas to learn of their freedom remains a mystery. Some say that the masters suppressed the news until they'd had time to harvest one last crop. Others claim that the soldier carrying the proclamation was killed along the route. Still others say word of freedom was carried by a messenger on the back of the mule, and the trip simply took him that long. Whatever the reason, you can be

*Hibiscus Tea Punch quenches everyone's
thirst with a blast of flavor and color.*

sure that the news was a cause for rejoicing. Just one year later, that day was remembered in the first Juneteenth celebration. The festivities were focused around baseball and barbecues.

Juneteenth became a huge holiday in the South, sometimes lasting a whole week. There were parades and floats, baseball games, square dancing, and calf roping. At some point, someone might read the Emancipation Proclamation, and everyone would join in singing "Amazing Grace." The day would end with a supper or dance that lasted until the early hours of the morning.

Since 1980, Juneteenth has been an official state holiday in Texas, and there are good-sized celebrations in other states, too. Just a few years ago, I saw my first Juneteenth celebration—in Connecticut. It was a big outdoor gathering, with heaps of picnic foods, plenty of entertainment and activities, and a wonderfully festive atmosphere.

Recently, when we were out at the house on Sag Harbor, I decided to throw a Juneteenth celebration for my friends. In keeping with the spirit of the occasion, I thought an outdoor barbecue would be fun. We gathered around a sturdy wooden table I'd covered in brightly colored kente cloth, and ate and talked the afternoon away.

Juneteenth feasting has traditionally centered around the barbecue. The idea is to soak up the same flavors and aromas that the freed slaves would have experienced during their first celebrations. In any case, barbecues give outdoor gatherings that festive, holiday feel; and I liked the idea of serving down-home foods at my Juneteenth picnic—the foods that we all grew up on, like barbecued ribs and grilled chicken.

They say that the foods of Juneteenth are traditionally red in color: People drank strawberry soda pop and ate red "emancipation" cake. I loved the idea of a meal being designed around a color, so I took the red theme and had fun with it. Along with the hibiscus tea punch, which is a really pretty red, I made my special red sweet maple barbecue sauce, which is slightly spicy, for the chicken and spare ribs, and served slices of watermelon for dessert. The crowning glory of this col-

orful feast was a red velvet layer cake—my take on the traditional emancipation cake. The black-eyed pea salad added a truly Southern touch.

  With all of that vibrant color, the smells wafting from the barbecue, and the special feeling that comes with relaxing among friends in the soft, open air of early summer, the picnic turned out just as I'd hoped. There were no readings of the proclamation, but I think we were all reminded how important it is to be truly free.

A Juneteenth Celebration

Black-eyed Pea Salad

Barbecued Chicken
and Spare Ribs
with B.'s Sweet Maple
Barbecue Sauce

Baked Sweet Potatoes

Cornbread

Red Velvet Cake

Hibiscus Tea Punch

Watermelon

*Our Juneteenth celebration features a
down-home barbecue including my very
own B.'s Sweet Maple Barbecue Sauce.
We gather outdoors and feast on (from
left) Baked Sweet Potatoes, Barbecued
Spare Ribs, Cornbread, and Black-eyed
Pea Salad.*

BLACK-EYED PEA SALAD

SERVES 8

3 tablespoons extra virgin olive oil

2 tablespoons balsamic vinegar

1¼ teaspoon ground cumin

1¼ teaspoon minced garlic

¾ teaspoon salt

½ teaspoon cayenne pepper

¼ cup finely chopped red onion

½ cup chopped red bell pepper

2 tablespoons chopped black olives

3 tablespoons chopped fresh basil leaves

2 tablespoons chopped pimientos

2 cups cooked long-grain white rice

2 cups cooked fresh or frozen black-eyed peas

8 cups salad greens

In a large bowl, whisk together the olive oil, vinegar, cumin, garlic, salt and cayenne pepper. Add the onion, bell pepper, olives, basil, pimientos, rice, and peas. Toss the salad enough to moisten. Cover and refrigerate up to 24 hours. Serve on a bed of salad greens.

BARBECUED CHICKEN

SERVES 8

8 pounds frying chicken, cut into pieces

½ cup vegetable oil

Salt and freshly ground black pepper to taste

B.'s Sweet Maple Barbecue Sauce
(recipe follows)

Wash and dry the chicken pieces. Coat with oil and season with salt and pepper on both sides. Prepare the grill (charcoal or gas) according to the manufacturer's directions for medium heat. Place the chicken on the grill, skin side down, and cook 10 minutes on each side. Brush each piece of chicken with the barbecue sauce, turn, and grill 10 to 12 minutes, or until cooked thoroughly (when juices run clear). Turn frequently to avoid burning, brushing with barbecue sauce as needed. The chicken should be tender and slightly charred to taste. Serve warm or at room temperature.

BARBECUED SPARE RIBS

SERVES 8

*6–8 pounds pork spare ribs
(approx. 3 slabs pork spare ribs)*
Salt and freshly ground black pepper to taste
*B.'s Sweet Maple Barbecue Sauce
(recipe follows)*

Preheat the oven to 350 degrees. Rinse the spare ribs in cold water and pat dry with a paper towel. Season the ribs with salt and pepper on both sides. Place the ribs in a large shallow roasting pan. Bake for 30 minutes. Turn the ribs over and continue to bake for another 30 minutes. Drain excess oil from the pan. Prepare the grill (charcoal or gas) according to the manufacturer's directions for medium heat. Brush each slab with barbecue sauce and grill 10 to 15 minutes. Turn frequently to avoid burning, brushing with barbecue sauce as needed. Serve warm or at room temperature.

B.'S SWEET MAPLE BARBECUE SAUCE

Yields 3–4 cups

2 tablespoons butter
1 medium onion, finely chopped
2 cloves garlic, minced
½ cup orange juice
1 cup vinegar
2 tablespoons lemon juice
2 slices lemon
1 cup maple syrup
¼ cup Worcestershire sauce
2 cups ketchup
2 tablespoons dry mustard
1 teaspoon salt
½ teaspoon crushed dried red pepper
½ teaspoon paprika

In a large saucepan, heat the butter. Add the onion and garlic, and cook over medium heat until softened. Add the remaining ingredients, stir and simmer for 30 minutes. Remove the lemon slices. The sauce will keep, covered and refrigerated, up to 2 weeks.

BAKED SWEET POTATOES

SERVES 8

8 medium sweet potatoes

Preheat the oven to 425 degrees. Clean the potatoes under running water, using a brush to remove dirt. Using a fork, poke several shallow holes into the potatoes to allow steam to escape. On a baking sheet, arrange the potatoes slightly apart. Bake 45 minutes. Test for doneness by piercing the potatoes with a thin skewer. Continue baking until the potatoes feel soft when squeezed, approximately 1 hour. Serve warm or at room temperature.

CORNBREAD

SERVES 8

2 cups cornmeal
1 cup all-purpose flour
3 teaspoons baking powder
1½ teaspoons salt
¼ cup sugar
1¼ cups milk
3 eggs
¾ cup (1½ sticks) melted butter

Preheat the oven to 400 degrees. Grease a 10-inch ovenproof cast-iron skillet. In a large bowl, combine the cornmeal, flour, baking powder, salt, and sugar. Stir in the milk, eggs, and butter, mixing just until the dry ingredients are moistened. Pour the batter into the skillet and bake 20 to 25 minutes, or until a toothpick inserted in the center comes out clean.

RED VELVET CAKE

SERVES 8

2 cups cake flour

3 tablespoons unsweetened cocoa powder

2 teaspoons baking powder

1 teaspoon salt

¾ cup (1½ sticks) butter, softened

1¾ cups sugar

4 large eggs

1 cup milk

3 teaspoons red food coloring

1 teaspoon vanilla extract

BUTTERCREAM FROSTING

6 cups powdered sugar

1 cup (2 sticks) butter, softened

4 to 6 tablespoons heavy cream

2 teaspoons vanilla extract

Preheat the oven to 350 degrees. Grease and flour two 9-inch cake pans. In a large bowl, stir together the flour, cocoa, baking powder, and salt. In another large bowl, cream together the butter and sugar until light and fluffy. Beat in the eggs one at a time. In a small bowl, combine the milk, food coloring, and vanilla. Using a spatula, fold into the egg mixture the flour mixture alternating with the liquids, ending with the dry ingredients. Pour the batter into the pans and bake about 30 to 35 minutes. Test with a toothpick until it comes out clean. Cool in the pans 5 minutes before turning out onto racks.

To make the frosting, mix all the ingredients together until light and fluffy.

When the cakes are completely cool, frost with Buttercream Frosting between the layers, on the sides, and on top of the cake.

HIBISCUS TEA PUNCH

SERVES 8

8 hibiscus or Red Zinger tea bags

4 cups boiling water

1½ cups sugar or honey

One 25.4-ounce bottle sparkling cider, chilled

Lemongrass or lemon wedges to garnish

Place the tea bags in a large container. Add the boiling water and let steep 10 minutes. Remove the tea bags; add the sugar or honey while the tea is hot. Refrigerate until ready to use. Add the sparkling cider. Serve in tall glasses over ice. Garnish with lemongrass or lemon wedges.

A Catered Party

June is a terrifically busy month for parties at our B. Smith restaurants. Everybody seems to be celebrating some kind of ending or beginning—or both. People throw wedding parties, end-of-school-year parties, bon voyage parties, retirement parties, graduation parties—and some of those new graduates are old enough to have grown-up children of their own. They are the celebrations I get the biggest kick out of. I really admire anyone who says, "I can do more with my life," and finds the time and energy to get a degree.

With everything going on at this time of year, many people prefer to hold their celebration parties at a restaurant. Though I'm the world's greatest fan of home entertaining, I agree that sometimes there are powerful arguments for letting someone else do all the work. Whether you're celebrating your graduation or your marriage, there's a lot to be said for spending those last few minutes before the guests arrive thinking about whether your lipstick needs a touch-up, rather than worrying about whether the roast will be overcooked or if there's enough soda. And when the last guests go home to relax, you can do the same.

Of course, when the party's all over, a catered affair is only going to feel like the perfect choice if everything turned out exactly the way you wanted it to. And for that to happen, you and the catering people you're working with need to communicate very clearly. You should describe exactly what you want, down to the last detail, and the restaurateur should explain what he or she is prepared to deliver. Otherwise, you might end up telling a party story like the one a friend of mine tells about her daughter's Sweet Sixteen bash.

My friend started out on the right track: She outlined a simple, teen-friendly menu for the chef. But when she started to sense that he considered her choices beneath his skills, she decided to let him express his creativity by leaving the selection of hors d'oeuvres up to him. Fortunately, the chef asked her to review the menu he planned to serve the teenagers, starting with curried chicken livers and duck confit fritters—not exactly the best choice for a hungry group of teenagers!

While I think that it's a good idea to let the chef make recommendations, remember that this is your party. Do what makes you comfortable, and serve what you think your guests will eat. Your party can be very elegant or very casual. You can tailor it to suit the occasion—but you have to ask yourself, and the person you're dealing with at the establishment, the right questions. Do you want a dance party? Do you want a band or a DJ? Are you able to decorate the space in advance? Would you prefer a buffet-style meal or sit-down service? And most important, can the restaurant provide these things? (For a complete list of questions you should ask, and things you should check into, see the following pages.)

When you're throwing a party in a restaurant or hall, it's always nice to give it your own personality, or the personality of the person who's being celebrated. If it's okay with the establishment, think about having some special decorations. You can buy special flowers or colored candles for the tables. When Dan and I got married and had our reception in the party room at B. Smith's restaurant, I bought several candle holders for the occasion. I kept them, and now bring them out for events whenever I feel like being sentimental.

Anything that individualizes the party will make the space feel more like yours. You could do something as simple as bringing in your own colored napkins, making a bouquet of balloons, or sprinkling candies or glitter in the center of each tabletop. (If you're throwing the party around Easter time, you might want to put bowls of jelly beans on the tables; if it's close to Valentine's Day, you could go for a red-hearts-and-chocolates theme.) I sometimes like to put a small gift at every place setting. Other options include a banner, place cards, or a guest book. You might even want to have special centerpieces made, or to make your own. Someone I know threw a party for a man who's into top hats. She bought several paper hats and placed them on the tables as centerpieces, with streamers flowing out of them.

HOW TO HAVE A RESTAURANT PARTY
THAT YOU'LL ENJOY LIKE A GUEST

When you're choosing the restaurant, your first concern should be the location. What neighborhood is convenient for the majority of your guests? Once you've narrowed down your choices to a particular area, your best bet is a place you've already sampled and enjoyed. Even if you don't think the place you have in mind has facilities for private parties, give them a call. Some of the regulars at B. Smith's in New York were not aware that we have a special room upstairs for private celebrations. If you don't have a restaurant in mind, get a referral from someone you trust.

If you have in mind a particular type of cuisine—say, Mexican or Italian food, possibly coinciding with a party theme—and the restaurant you like best specializes in something different, ask if the kitchen can put together the type of meal you want. Also, if you'd like a particular dish served, you might find that the chef is willing to work from your recipe.

In general, you'll find that the more accommodating an establishment is willing to be, the happier your experience will be.

Before you make a visit, rule out places that aren't suitable. If a large enough room isn't available for the date of your event, if the place isn't within reach of your budget, or if there's no way to set up a dance floor and you're looking forward to dancing, don't waste a trip. Call ahead first and ask about all of the following:

- capacity of rooms available

- times of day rooms are available (plus time limit, if any)

- availability of an appropriate room for your chosen date

- approximate range of total per-person costs

- whether a minimum number of guests must be guaranteed

- whether a deposit is required

- whether there's a dance floor, room for a band, any restrictions on live music (if these are what you have planned)

If you get the answers you want to these questions, you could ask for a suggested menu and wine lists to be mailed or faxed.

At your first meeting, you should have an estimate of the number of guests you expect. Also, you need to decide whether you want a buffet-type meal or sit-down service. Look at the room, decide if you like the ambiance, and get answers to these questions:

- How will the tables be set up?

- If there will be more than one party going on, what is the arrangement? How is privacy ensured?

- What arrangements are there for coat check?

- What are the terms of payment: amount of deposit, schedule for payments, and forms of payment?

- What is the policy regarding refunds?

To be perfectly clear about food, drink, and service, make sure you've provided all the information about the type of meal you want. Ask to see a detailed menu, including the number and kinds of hors d'oeuvres and if they will be passed or stationary. Ask the following questions:

- Can you bring your own dessert or cake, and is there a cutting charge?

- Can you have a tasting beforehand of the foods that will be served?

- What kind of serving dishes will be used?

- How will platters be garnished?

- Will plates be cleared when guests return to a buffet? Before the dessert is served?

- Will coffee and tea be served with dessert?

- What is the ratio of staff to guests? (An ideal ratio is 1:12 for a sit-down dinner, or 1:18 for a buffet.)

- What is the total cost for service? Are gratuities and tax included?

- What are the costs for the bar?

- How long will the bar remain open?

If you are renting a hall or other facility, look at the cooking facilities. If they seem fine, you'll probably want to be clear about some small but far from unimportant details:

- Who does the cleanup?

- What kind of security is offered?

- Are there any restrictions on the catering?

- Is there a rental fee for linens, china, glass, and flatware?

Other details to consider, whether you're looking at a hall or restaurant:

- Is parking available? What is the cost of valet parking?

- When can a florist come in? Is the florist included in the cost of the event?

- If you're planning to have a band, are there sufficient electrical outlets and a microphone?

If you will be hiring a DJ or musicians, get references and ask where the person or group has played in the past. You might even want to audition the performers or ask for a tape from the DJ. Ask specific questions about whether the person or group can play the type of music, and even the songs, that you want. Here's what you're trying to find out: Does the DJ have the right tapes, CDs, and/or records? Will the band play the classics or mostly showcase its own material? (Expect an invitation to provide a list of songs you do want to hear and any others you would like omitted from the play list.) Then check the following:

- How many musicians and what type of equipment will you be getting?

- Can they fill a room of your size with sound?

- Will there be lights or special effects? Is there an extra fee for that?

- Are the musicians willing to adhere to a requested dress code?

- Are they willing to act as emcees (if you want them to)?

- Will the band play if members of the family or friends want to sing? (If they say no, don't hire them)

- Are you expected to provide dinner, lodging, or transportation for the band?

- What is the fee? How many hours (and how many breaks) will that include? Will there be prerecorded music to cover breaks?

- Will they stay overtime? For how long? What will that cost?

- How many people does the band intend to bring with them?

- What are the arrangements for the deposit, the balance, and payment for overtime?

- What is needed for setup: How many hours should the room be available beforehand? What kind of electrical outlets, adapters, and mikes are required?

- Is there a grace period for cancellations?

- What if the band breaks up or a member can't play?

JULY

We celebrate the Fourth of July, as we do every
other summer weekend, at our home in Sag
Harbor. The town looks picture perfect with red, white, and blue
flags hanging from porches; and on the big evening, it seems as if
every last person is having a party on the beach, a barbecue in the
yard, or a picnic—capped off by town fireworks.

Like everyone else in town, we throw a big party. Usually we
invite everybody over for a barbecue, but this year I decided that
for a change it would be much more fun to have a crab boil. I've
always liked creating new traditions, and seafood seems like a perfect, light choice for a hot summer day. This simple feast makes for
a special experience because it's so unusual, and it's a piece of old-
time Americana—perfect for July Fourth.

I settled on a combination of spicy boiled crabs and shrimp.
To round out the seafood, I served crusty bread and mounds of
local vegetables.

When most people hear the name "the Hamptons," they think of summering celebrities and beautiful beaches. I wish more people knew about the area's wonderful farms. It's true that many former potato fields are now the landscaped grounds of grand summer residences, but there are still quite a few local growers. By July, roadside stands are overflowing with flowers and fresh produce. So I didn't have to travel far to find firm, Red Bliss potatoes and just-picked ears of corn for my holiday feast.

Part of the fun—and the flavor—of a crab boil comes from the fact that you cook everything in one pot, so the tastes transfer from one food to the other, and all the foods take on the same spicy Creole seasoning. You start with a big pot of boiling, seasoned water. First, you throw in the potatoes because they take the longest to cook, then the corn, which sweetens the water. The crabs and the shrimp come last.

I'm not sure if crab boils are more fun to prepare or to eat. It's the ultimate no-frills meal, especially if you serve it the old-fashioned way: in the shell, on a table covered in newspaper. (I used the sports pages for a little extra amusement.) Cracking the shells and piling a huge mess of them all over the paper is all part of the experience.

I put small bowls of melted sweet butter on the table, along with a huge bowl filled to overflowing with boiled potatoes and corn on the cob. Served this way, the vegetables had that appetizing straight-from-the-field look. Because some people like to sample the Creole spices, I also put a couple of dishes of the seasoning on the table for people to dip into. To wash down our meal and offset the heat of the fiery spices, I served icy cold Red Stripe and an assortment of other beers.

Later, we went down to Main Street to observe the local custom of visiting an ice cream parlor for a pre-fireworks treat. Licking our cones, we debated among ourselves: Should we go to our friend's loft, wander over to the deck of our restaurant, or head back to our own backyard to see the great show in the sky?

A July Fourth Crab Boil for Eight

Spicy Crab and Shrimp Boil
with Boiled New Potatoes and
Corn on the Cob with Herbed Butter

Patchwork Brownies

Crusty breads
Assorted beers

Our July Fourth table is set with all the fixings for a Spicy Crab and Shrimp Boil.

SPICY CRAB AND SHRIMP BOIL

SERVES 8

32 live blue claw crabs

5 gallons water

6 tablespoons crab-and-shrimp boil seasoning or Old Bay Seasoning

3 whole cloves garlic, peeled

2 tablespoons cayenne pepper

Coarse salt

4 bay leaves

2 lemons, quartered

2 large onions, peeled, halved

2 pounds new red potatoes

5 ribs celery, trimmed and cut into 4-inch lengths

8 ears corn, shucked

2 pounds medium unshelled raw shrimp

Herbed Butter (recipe follows)

Rinse the crabs carefully under cold water.

In a large pot, over high heat, bring the water to a boil. Add the crab and shrimp boil or Old Bay Seasoning, garlic, cayenne pepper, salt, bay leaves, lemon, and onions to the boiling water. Boil 10 minutes. Add the potatoes and celery, and boil until the potatoes are crisp but tender. Remove the potatoes to a large platter. Cover to keep warm. Add the corn to the boiling water and cook until the corn is bright yellow, about 6 minutes. Remove the corn with tongs and keep warm. Return the water to a boil. Add the crabs in three batches and cook about 10 minutes, until the crabs turn bright pink and their legs can be easily pulled from the sockets. Return the water to a boil, add the shrimp, and cook until they turn pink, about 4 to 5 minutes. Transfer the vegetables and seafood to separate serving bowls and serve immediately with Herbed Butter.

HERBED BUTTER

Use your favorite herbs or spices to make flavored butter. Roll the softened butter into cylinders and wrap with plastic wrap or foil. Use within 24 hours or keep frozen about a month.

4 tablespoons finely chopped fresh parsley, oregano, and thyme or herbs of your choice

1 cup (2 sticks) butter, at room temperature

Chop the herbs finely. Add to the soft butter and mix well. Refrigerate in a small container with a cover until ready to use. Bring to room temperature before using.

PATCHWORK BROWNIES

YIELDS 24 BROWNIES

2 cups all-purpose flour

1 teaspoon baking powder

¼ teaspoon salt

1 cup (2 sticks) unsalted butter, at room temperature

1½ cups packed brown sugar

4 large eggs

2 teaspoons vanilla extract

Two 3-ounce bars Godiva dark chocolate, chopped

4 squares (4 ounces) unsweetened chocolate, chopped and melted

½ cup granulated sugar

Two 3-ounce bars Godiva ivory white chocolate, chopped

Preheat the oven to 350 degrees. Line a 13 × 9 × 2-inch baking pan with foil; grease the foil. Sift flour, baking powder, and salt into a small bowl. In a large bowl, with the electric mixer on medium speed, beat the butter and brown sugar until fluffy. Beat in two eggs and the vanilla. Beat in the dry ingredients until blended. Remove 1½ cups of the batter to a medium bowl. Add the dark chocolate to the batter remaining in the large bowl. Add the remaining eggs, melted chocolate, sugar, and white chocolate to a medium bowl. Stir well until blended.

Drop alternating teaspoonfuls of the batters into a prepared pan until all the batter is used. Bake 30 to 35 minutes, until a toothpick inserted in center comes out clean. (Note: If toothpick is inserted directly into chocolate it will not be clean.) Let cool completely on a wire rack. Lift from the pan by the foil; cut into 24 brownies.

A SUMMER SANDWICH PICNIC

It's hard for me to think of a meal I anticipated more eagerly as a child than the packed lunches my mom used to make for us when we went on car trips, whether we were going to the lake for a swim or just driving for a few hours to visit relatives. In those days, before you could find fast-food stands tucked away by the side of even the most rural road, we had to bring our own food—or go hungry. No quick snack will ever measure up to those lunches. I'm not sure whether the sandwiches were really as delicious as I remember, or if I enjoyed them so much because they were part of an exciting family ritual. After all, the menu was often nothing more exotic than peanut butter and jelly or egg salad.

I'm sure most families share this ritual; at some point during the summer, everyone packs up some sandwiches, some beverages, paper napkins, maybe even a table and chairs and a few games, and relocates their lunch or dinner to some outdoor spot. The main goal might be to swim or play ball; or it might be to enjoy a meal in the open air.

Sometimes we take a basket of goodies with us to a concert under the stars in Sag Harbor. I always enjoy these concerts, but for real pizzazz, nothing beats the free, open-air summer events in New York City's Central Park, which attract picnickers by the drove. Whether there's opera, symphonic music, or Paul Simon on the bill, I think these are among the greatest events that New York has to offer. They give me the chance to combine three of the things I enjoy the most: food, music, and the company of others.

If you haven't been there, the scene is almost impossible to imagine: Thousands of people, blanket to blanket, sitting peacefully in the heart of the world's busiest metropolis; a sea of city dwellers in a huge, cool oasis of green. People sprawl on blankets, some nestled beside a companion, some watching their kids play nearby or gazing up at the starlit sky.

We have those who lived in the Victorian era to thank for inventing the picnic. They may have a reputation for being straight-laced, but they knew how to indulge themselves. They created gadgets for every type of kitchen need, from grape shears to stuffing spoons to pickle forks, and they loved the foods that went along with these tools. Their picnics were stylish affairs that combined fine dining and the celebration of nature: You were supposed to take in the fantastic view while you ate, but the meal and its accoutrements got as much attention as the perspective. Picnic hampers were elaborate things, outfitted with linens and crystals and separated into little compartments, into which abundant amounts of food were packed.

Silver and linen might be overdoing it for a picnic today, but I think an elegant picnic basket is a great way to add some style to a ritual that most of us now associate with coolers. I used to buy antique baskets, paint them, and line them with a crisp cotton fabric; but now that picnic baskets are all the rage again, you can find them in kitchen and department stores in a great variety of styles. I once was invited to a picnic at which each guest was given a combination backpack–picnic basket that had compartments for all the ingredients that make up a perfect meal, including a bottle of wine and a corkscrew. The feast included a delicious pâté and crusty bread.

It's the food, of course, that really makes the picnic. Today's sandwiches are far removed from the ones I grew up with. Even a little while ago, sandwiches came on white bread and (if you were lucky) whole wheat. Now even the most remote little town seems to offer an array of choices: baguettes, whole grain, oatmeal, and focaccia. Sandwich fillings have changed, too. In fact these days, when you can get turkey and tuna sandwiches and even chicken wraps and vegetarian fillings pretty much anywhere, you have to be inventive to come up with sandwich ideas that are a little bit special, as well as flavorful, substantial, and nourishing.

Some people who want to do something different decide against sandwiches altogether. But for my picnic on the beach, I wanted to come up with some new ideas for fillings. Sandwiches have a lot going for them when you're bringing lunch for an outdoorsy trip: They can be prepared in advance, they're designed to be transported, and they're easy to eat. All you need is cool drinks and chips to make an afternoon meal everybody likes.

There's no end to the variety of great sandwiches you can invent if you keep certain things in mind. The first is choice; you want to make sure that there's something for everyone. I chose four different types of bread for my sandwiches, so that all of my guests would have something they liked. Think of foods that taste good at room temperature. I'd always had hot breaded fish sandwiches until I went to the Caribbean, where they serve them barely warm. For my picnic, I put breaded catfish between pieces of coarse whole-grain bread. The textures of the bread and the filling matched each other perfectly—another thing to consider when you're coming up with new sandwich ideas. Try different seasonings; something unusual, like tamarind, can make even chicken on a kaiser roll exciting. Use foods you usually serve on plates at the table. I put a slab of collard frittata between two slices of focaccia for an unusual type of egg sandwich. And think about how the bread holds the filling. Pita bread, which is also called pocket bread, was just the right "container" for a lump crab filling with sprouts.

Like the sandwiches, the Key lime tartlets I served for dessert are finger food. Their heavy crust holds them together for traveling; you just have to double wrap them to protect the custardy filling. At the beach, I arranged them and the sandwiches in a large, flat basket, together with some natural treasures for decoration—seashells and starfish. The scene was complete.

Some favorite summer sandwiches.
They make a great treat for the beach,
the park, or any other fun destination.

A Summer Sandwich Picnic for Four

Tamarind-Spiced Chicken Sandwich

Crab and Avocado Salad in a Pita

Pan-Fried Catfish and Ginger Slaw
on Whole-Grain Bread

Collard Greens
Frittata Sandwich

Dan's Key Lime Tartlets

Assorted flavored iced teas

TAMARIND-SPICED CHICKEN SANDWICH

SERVES 4

2 tablespoons lime juice

2 tablespoons olive oil

2 tablespoons unsweetened tamarind paste

2 tablespoons molasses

3 cloves garlic, minced

4 skinless boneless chicken breast halves

Salt and freshly ground black pepper to taste

4 romaine lettuce leaves

4 kaiser rolls

¼ cup each diced red and yellow bell pepper

2 teaspoons grated lime zest

In a small bowl, whisk together the lime juice, olive oil, tamarind paste, molasses, and garlic. Season the chicken breasts with salt and pepper, and place in a heavy-duty sealable plastic bag. Pour the marinade over chicken, seal the bag, and marinate at least 2 hours.

Heat an outdoor grill or use a grill pan on the stove. Remove the chicken from the marinade. Grill chicken over medium-high heat 5 to 6 minutes on each side, until cooked through. Set aside to cool.

Diagonally slice chicken breasts. Arrange a lettuce leaf on the bottom half of each of the four kaiser rolls. Top with sliced chicken, diced bell pepper, lime zest, and kaiser roll tops. Wrap the sandwiches in waxed paper and keep chilled until ready to serve.

CRAB AND AVOCADO SALAD IN A PITA

SERVES 4

⅔ cup mayonnaise

2 tablespoons diced roasted red bell pepper

4 tablespoons lemon juice

Pinch ground cayenne pepper

2 cups lump crabmeat, picked through for shells

1 small avocado, peeled and chopped

2 tablespoons grated onion

Salt and ground white pepper to taste

4 white or whole wheat pita pocket-breads

1 cup alfalfa sprouts

In a blender, puree the mayonnaise, roasted pepper, 1 tablespoon of the lemon juice, and the cayenne pepper. Set aside. In a medium bowl, toss together the crabmeat, avocado, onion, remaining lemon juice, the salt, and pepper.

Cut the top third off the pitas. Divide the crabmeat mixture among the pitas, drizzle with red pepper mayonnaise, and tuck alfalfa sprouts into each sandwich. Tightly wrap in waxed paper and keep chilled up to 1 hour.

PAN-FRIED CATFISH AND GINGER SLAW ON WHOLE-GRAIN BREAD

SERVES 4

4 catfish fillets (or whiting)

Salt and freshly ground black pepper to taste

1 cup yellow cornmeal

3 tablespoons vegetable oil

8 slices whole-grain bread

4 tablespoons mayonnaise

4 lettuce leaves

Ginger Slaw (recipe follows)

Rinse the fish and wipe with paper toweling. Season with salt and pepper. Dip fish in cornmeal to coat both sides. Heat the oil in a large skillet over medium heat; cook the fish until browned, about 3 minutes. Carefully turn the fish and cook about 3 minutes longer until cooked through. Drain the fish on a wire rack lined with paper toweling.

Spread 4 of the bread slices with mayonnaise, then top each with a lettuce leaf and fish fillet. Put a large spoonful of Ginger Slaw on each fillet and top with the remaining bread slices. Wrap each sandwich tightly in waxed paper and keep chilled until ready to serve.

GINGER SLAW

¾ cup shredded green cabbage

¾ cup shredded red cabbage

½ cup coarsely grated carrot

1 tablespoon finely chopped crystallized ginger

2 teaspoons lime juice

¼ teaspoon salt

3–4 tablespoons mayonnaise

In a medium bowl toss together all ingredients except the mayonnaise. Stir in the mayonnaise, then refrigerate at least 1 hour before serving.

COLLARD GREENS FRITATTA SANDWICH

SERVES 4

3 tablespoons olive oil

1 cup diced potatoes

1 small onion, chopped

2 cloves garlic, minced

1½ cups cooked collard greens, well drained

¼ teaspoon crushed red pepper

8 large eggs, beaten

½ teaspoon salt

¼ teaspoon freshly ground black pepper

⅓ cup grated Parmesan cheese

1 round loaf country white bread, 10 inches in diameter

1 large ripe beefsteak tomato, sliced

In a 10-inch ovenproof skillet, preferably nonstick, heat the olive oil. Add the potatoes and cook, stirring frequently, over medium heat 5 to 6 minutes. Add the onion and garlic; continue cooking until the potatoes are golden brown and the onion is wilted. Stir in the collard greens and crushed red pepper.

Preheat the oven to 350 degrees. Season the beaten eggs with the salt and pepper. Pour over the potato-collard mixture and cook over low heat until the eggs are almost set, 8 to 10 minutes. Sprinkle the frittata with the Parmesan. Transfer the skillet to the oven and bake 4 to 5 minutes, until the top of the frittata is set and the cheese is melted. Set aside to cool.

Split the round country loaf in half horizontally. Place the cooled frittata on the bottom half of the bread. Arrange the tomato slices on the frittata and top with the other half of the bread. Cut sandwich in 4 wedges and wrap in waxed paper. Keep cool until ready to serve.

DAN'S KEY LIME TARTLETS

My husband loves Key lime pie and I created this version with a sturdy walnut crust that could travel to a picnic. Be sure to keep tartlets chilled before serving.

MAKES 4 INDIVIDUAL TARTLETS OR ONE 9-INCH PIE

PIE SHELL

1 cup crushed graham crackers (about 20 squares)

½ cup brown sugar

½ cup ground walnuts

¼ teaspoon ground cinnamon

¼ teaspoon ground nutmeg

⅓ cup melted butter

FILLING

4 large egg yolks

One 4-ounce can sweetened condensed milk

¼ cup fresh-squeezed lime juice (preferably from Key limes)

2 teaspoons freshly grated lime zest

Lime zest for garnish

To make the pie shell, preheat the oven to 350 degrees. In a medium bowl, stir together the graham cracker crumbs, sugar, walnuts, cinnamon, and nutmeg. Add the melted butter and mix until well blended. Press evenly onto the bottom and sides of four 4-inch tartlet plates or one 9-inch pie plate. Bake 10 minutes, until golden. Remove from the oven and let cool completely. Do not turn off the oven.

To make the filling, in a medium bowl, beat together the egg yolks, condensed milk, lime juice, and grated zest until blended. Pour the filling into the pie shell. Bake 12 to 15 minutes, or until the center of the pie is set. Let cool completely on a rack; refrigerate until cold. Garnish with lime zest.

AUGUST

A Family Reunion

We didn't do many "official" family reunions when I was growing up, but in the summer there were always family members coming to town on visits. Our family reunions usually happened in August, when our relatives gathered for the Baptist Homecoming celebration. If we didn't run into one of the visitors at the homecoming meal, we'd be likely to see them at my grandmother's house. So at least once a year we'd have a visit from Aunt Vert and Auntie Gertrude and Little Jessie, along with lots of other family members and friends who had come back home from New York and Philadelphia or traveled up from North Carolina.

As a person who loves ritual and the flow of memory, I'm all for the idea of family reunions. I think today, when so many of us live far from our relatives and events like homecomings are dying

Remember to take a family portrait each time you gather
for a reunion. You'll treasure it for years to come.

*Sharing a special
moment between
generations*

out, reunions are more important than ever. When family ties have to stretch over long distances, they become fragile. Maybe people are starting to miss that feeling of being part of something that goes way back, because these days family reunions seem to be growing more and more popular.

What I like about these affairs is that they celebrate every single family member who is there, from the matriarchs and patriarchs who can tell stories about their grandparents on down to the children who'll carry these stories into the future. And since no one in particular is hosting the event, there's no limit to the number of people who can be part of it.

I've organized family-reunion-type events for many people, and over the years I've learned what makes them fun. My suggestions in this chapter are based on what I've learned in my work; some of the ideas evolved from a weekend reunion I attended in my hometown, organized by a group of my relatives. They put a lot of time and energy into planning things so that everybody would go back home feeling happy and enriched. It's up to you to adapt the ideas you'll find here so that they suit you and your family.

The whole idea of holding this type of reunion is to bring the extended family together, usually for a weekend and on common ground. (You might even include "family"—those people who as a child you called aunt or uncle, even though they weren't related to you.) It's a way of defining who this family is, and an opportunity for each member to define who he or she is in relation to the group.

I think there's a certain part of each of us that wants to search our roots so we can figure out why we are who we are. The reunion is an occasion for the sharing of stories that fill in the family picture for everyone. When I get together with my aunt and uncle in Washington, I always find out something about the family that I didn't know before. Hearing these stories helps me feel connected. Your lifestyle might be completely different from the lifestyles of other family members, but there's still that thread of shared experience and a common history.

As the person organizing the reunion, your job is to make the event as stress-free as possible for everyone, with plenty of opportunities for people to mingle across the generations. You want family members who might not have seen one another for years to be able to relax and enjoy one another's company. It takes a lot of thoughtful planning, down to the last detail. And, as someone who's planned weekends of this type, I can tell you that taking care of the details for a large group of people, old and young, is a monumental job. But in the process of working to bring everybody together in one place, you might learn some interesting things about your family or possibly discover a long-lost relative.

The first thing I recommend to anyone who's about to embark on this mission is that they lighten their workload by forming a committee of volunteers to help. You don't need experts—any relative who's enthusiastic about the idea will do (although if anyone in the family has experience in event planning, you'll want to use all your powers of persuasion to get them involved). In a committee, everyone can pool their expertise. And the bigger your core group, the more family members you'll be likely to reach. These days, if you have access to e-mail and a fax machine, it doesn't even matter how close to you your committee members live.

Give yourselves plenty of lead time to plan. The work itself is time-consuming. Also, popular hotels and restaurants tend to book up months or even years in advance, especially during the summer months.

You'll need to decide on the best time to get the family together. Holding the reunion off-season may give you more options and cut costs. You might think about having it in autumn, which can be very beautiful in many parts of the country. Christmas is usually a time for celebrating at home, but some

It's hard to not have a good time at a family reunion. Remembering old times together always makes people laugh.

family members might welcome the idea of gathering in a restaurant in a different city—on neutral territory. Still, most people decide to hold their reunions in August for obvious reasons: Kids are off from school, it's a slow time for businesses and so a convenient time for most adults to take vacations, and there are no snowstorms or hurricanes to sabotage travel plans.

Next, you'll have to decide where to hold the reunion. Obviously, the easiest place is in the town where you live; you'll have an easier time checking out facilities for reunion events. But while your hometown may seem like a logical choice, I think it can be a good idea to hold the reunion in a place that also happens to be a popular tourist spot. For a start, you'll have available plenty of suitable hotel rooms and restaurants and a wide choice of activities to keep people busy. And if the site is appealing, more people are likely to come.

Personally, I think Washington, D.C., is an ideal place for a reunion. It's such a great tourist town, it's relatively easy to get to, and I find it as interesting as any other city in this country. It has a little bit of something for everyone, yet it's a lot more manageable than New York or Los Angeles.

The average family reunion attracts about fifty people, and most of those people will need accommodations. When you're trying to find places that are suitable for out-of-town visitors, don't just look into the obvious hotels and motels. You might find a perfect supply of modestly priced rooms in condo communities, camps, conference centers, lodges, even college dorms. A smallish group might even take over an entire bed-and-breakfast. (If you fill all the rooms, the host may give you a discount and make a special effort to be accommodating.) A friend of mine did this for a wedding party, and it was a huge success.

Most B&Bs were at one time private homes, so they have an intimate, comfortable feel. If you want to prepare a meal communally, you might find that the kitchen is big enough to accommodate you. Even if you're holding a large reunion, a B&B could be the "hub" facility where the committee stays, and which serves as a kind of information/hospitality center. You could set up a bulletin board as a communications center and have coffee and soft drinks available all day long for informal gatherings. You might even be able to use the grounds for an event or two.

The events are the essence of any reunion. When I think back to my own family reunion, I remember most vividly the meals we shared and

Dessert gets everyone's attention, especially the kids'.

the planned activities. All the eating together, playing together, working together—and posing for photos together—helped each of us get a sense of where and how we fit into the big picture of the family.

If you have a weekend reunion, figure on having at least four planned events: a Friday night supper, lunch and activities on Saturday afternoon, a dress-up party on Saturday night, and some sort of send-off event for Sunday.

Keep Friday night casual so people don't feel intimidated when they first see each other after a while. Cooking and working together is a great ice-breaker. Friday night fish fries were a tradition in my family. My mother would cook whiting, catfish, shrimp, and curried fried oysters along with french fries, coleslaw, chili mayonnaise, and Creole tartar sauce. You'll need a community kitchen where you can prepare the meal: Check out the local American Legion hall, a school cafeteria, even a vineyard. Don't hesitate to contact churches, too. They're often willing to rent their facilities.

A friend of mine had the idea of renting one of the buildings at a local museum—actually a restored nineteenth-century village with some new public

REUNION TIPS

If you're planning on a single event, you can probably pull a reunion together in six months. But if you're planning a big blowout weekend, allow a year to eighteen months (especially eighteen months if you're doing it for the first time). It will take awhile just to get a current address list together.

Arrange for the various committee members to share the burden of start-up costs, which might include postage and deposits for halls and catering. You can ultimately recoup these expenses by including some sort of "registration fee" in the charge for the reunion. The fee might even include the cost of a reunion souvenir like a T-shirt or baseball cap.

Offer a discount for early registration to get people going.

If people are traveling some distances, a travel agent may work with you to get group rates on airfares and hotels, and to coordinate ground transportation and other details. Before you call, have an idea of your per-person budget. Remember to present any special requests for car rentals or sightseeing. When you contact family members to announce the reunion, include the travel agent's fax or e-mail number and/or toll-free phone number.

Contact the Chamber of Commerce of the city where you're holding the reunion. They may be able to provide you with booklets, maps, or other items. A large city may also have a Convention and Visitors Bureau that gives you everything from printed information to free coupons and other promotional items, and may also help you in other areas, from finding restaurants to lodging.

Hold a yard sale and use the proceeds to purchase something in the family name—plant a tree marked with a plaque, donate a brick at a local college or a seat in the concert hall or community theater, give books with nameplates to the church or local school. Or make a gift to charity.

---

buildings—and hired a company to put up a tent outside. If the nights are balmy, and there's a park or beach where you can set up a grill, you could all get together for an outdoor barbecue. The main point is to focus on familiar foods that everybody feels comfortable with: barbecued chicken and ribs, potato salad and coleslaw, hot dogs and hamburgers, and an assortment of homestyle desserts.

If your family isn't the type to enjoy spending time in the kitchen, I'm sure you'll be able to find a restaurant that's willing to do a special meal for you. Don't hesitate to ask for a special dish, even if it is not on the menu. At B. Smith's, we have done special fish fries and waffle-and-chicken lunches for reunion committees many times.

Every family seems to have someone who is the obvious choice for master of ceremonies. Your fun-loving Aunt Emma or Uncle Henry can give the event a focus, set the tone, and act as a kind of "leader" for the events. My friend's husband was asked to fill this role at his family gathering. He wore a top hat and

WHEN YOU SEND OUT THE ANNOUNCE-MENTS Ask who might like to sing a song, play an instrument, or recite a poem written for the occasion. These performances can be part of the Friday or Saturday night festivities.

Ask everyone to nominate themselves for an award in any category in which they consider themselves special. Tell them the categories can range from serious to silly: Oldest, Traveled Furthest to Reunion, Most Grandchildren, Best Hair, Strangest Musical Talent, Weirdest Occupation, Most Degrees, Biggest Foot, and so on. Make the "awards ceremony" part of the fun on Friday or Saturday night. (You can buy medals from a trophy shop, or make your own, to add to the fun.)

Ask people to send or bring family recipes. Reproduce them and distribute them at the reunion or afterward.

Have each person or family fill out a page listing names and ages of immediate family members, phone numbers and addresses, and a short biography of each. Reproduce these, bind them into a booklet, and distribute them at the reunion.

Send everyone a set of ten index cards to be used at the reunion in a game of "Family Trivia." Ask them to volunteer questions and answers.

Ask people to send photographs for a family tree. (Have them write their names and addresses on the back if they want the photos returned.) Reprint the family tree for distribution at the reunion.

AT THE REUNION Put up a bulletin board displaying the family tree, along with the photos people sent.

If you plan a Friday night cook-out, find a volunteer for chief cook, someone to coordinate the ingredients and supplies, and someone to recruit and supervise people for KP duty and cleanup.

Find a volunteer to be the "official cinematographer." This person should document the whole event and include still photos and other memorabilia, interviews with the oldest members of the family, and so on. Copies can be made for family members to order.

tails, gave an official speech of welcome at the Friday night dinner, and introduced some of the "notables" in the crowd—the oldest family members and the most distant relatives, as well as people who lived far away and didn't know many of the others. When he coaxed some of them to stand up and share their recollections from the past, there was plenty of laughter along with a few tears.

On Saturday, plan on letting people get up at leisure, make their own arrangements for breakfast, and do some exploring or visiting. Then plan a lunchtime get-together and an afternoon of fun. If you're in a city like Washington, there's almost no limit to the type of excursions you can plan, but every place offers some kind of sightseeing adventure for which you can charter a bus.

My family's Saturday afternoon outdoor games event was a huge success, because it gave everybody the freedom to be totally silly. There are lots of laughs to be had when a group of people of different sizes and shapes get together to play games like horseshoes, softball, tug of war, relay races, or steal the bacon. In

Family reunions help strengthen bonds with those we seldom see.

case the weather doesn't go along with your plans, have equipment ready for indoor games—bingo, cards, and board games—and arts and crafts for the children.

When you send out your announcements for the reunion, ask people to bring some of their old family photographs. They'll come in handy when you all get together to work on a family history project. This is when the elders in the family really blossom. They can help fill in the blanks if you decide to draw the family tree (with identifying photos) or tape an oral history. Other family members may be able to identify some of the "mystery" characters who appear in some of the pictures. Expect to get lots of requests for copies of the photos. Even if they're in bad condition, they can be rephotographed or videotaped for posterity.

Every family reunion should have one formal dinner-dance party so everyone has an opportunity to enjoy one another's company while they're all dressed up; I've always found that people are different when they're in formal dress. You'll probably plan this for Saturday evening at a restaurant or hotel. (See page 114 for tips on holding a catered party.) A party boat would make a great venue, if one is available in your area.

To accommodate a variety of diets and tastes, be sure to plan a menu that offers a choice of poultry, fish, meat, or a vegetarian main course. (In the packet you send people listing the events and fees, you may want them to indicate a choice of entrée in advance. This will allow you to get a better price from a restaurant or caterer, since just the right amount of each food can be ordered.) You could start the evening with a cocktail hour. Have a couple of hors d'oeuvres stations set up so people can hang out before sitting down to dinner.

You might decide to start dinner off with a speech, or with the saying of grace. One of my friends asked her hundred-year-old great-great-grandmother to say grace before the formal dinner at her family reunion. Whether a prayer or a toast feels more right for you and your family, these moments of composure before the meal begins help focus everyone on the experience of being gathered together under one roof.

I think it's a good idea to leave everyone to their own devices for Sunday breakfast. If you wish, you can arrange to gather at a local church for Sunday services or, to make the day very special, perhaps you can have a member of the clergy conduct a private service.

With the family all gathered together and everybody in a thoroughly senti-mental mood after a weekend of memories, this would be a perfect occasion for one or more couples to renew their wedding vows. (You'll find ideas for this cer-emony on page 145.)

To follow the morning service, I can't imagine a better choice than a bar-becue. Everybody likes food cooked on a grill, and a hearty meal is a great send-off for the trip home. There's a wonderful camaraderie about working together with people you love, to prepare food for the other people you love (and with all those feelings of love, surely you'll find volunteers to help with the cleanup!).

Before everyone leaves, hold a family meeting. Take a vote on when and where to have the next reunion, and decide who will be in charge. And don't for-get to take a family picture. One family I know has created a ritual around the annual reunion photo, with everyone posing in a pyramid organized by weight. The heaviest stand at the bottom; the lightest perch on top. It's funny to look back at the pictures over the years and see various family members "dropping down."

When the reunion's over, these are the things—the photos, the stories, the memories—that will make the job of organizing the event seem more than worthwhile.

A Renewal of Wedding Vows Ceremony

To me, a renewal of vows is an even more meaningful celebration than the original marriage ceremony. Love that endures over time is the real thing.

A renewal ceremony can be anything you want it to be—casual or formal, lighthearted or serious, brief and simple or a chance to party. You can incorporate it into a family reunion or have an intimate setting and invite your closest friends. You might want to encourage other couples to plan a joint ceremony with you. If they prefer, they can simply stand up along with you for a vow-renewal reading.

The first time you get married, the rules are pretty well spelled out for you, starting with who conducts the service. I used to love the old movies about shipboard romance, with the captain of the ship marrying the couple, but in real life you're usually stuck with a more conventional choice when you want to make your union legal. When you renew your vows, you can choose whomever you want to officiate—and in my mind, that's the person who'll best put your sentiments into words. It might be a family member who went to divinity school but isn't necessarily ordained, someone who expresses himself or herself like a poet, or someone who *is* a poet.

You could ask the most senior member of the family to add some comments, and perhaps your children will want to say a few words. The ceremony doesn't have to be entirely solemn if solemn isn't your style. You might want to have it conducted by someone who knows both of you well enough to have fun.

This is your chance to dream up a perfect wedding ceremony. If there are any would-be flower girls or boys at your ceremony, you could give them their chance to dress up and carry baskets of petals. The "bridesmaids" could color-coordinate their outfits, wear matching ribbons, or hold matching flowers. And the "re-bride"—the one who's becoming a bride a second time—could wear white shorts if she felt in the mood!

If you didn't have the big white wedding the first time around, you might want to go all out with the dress and tux. Or you might want to put on the wedding outfits you wore the first time around—if they still fit!

Family and friends look on as Dan and I renew our vows.

SEPTEMBER

A Labor Day Weekend Dinner Party

If I could choose my own personal New Year's Day, I'd schedule it for September. Although there's a part of me that would be happy living somewhere in an eternal summer, another part looks forward to that feeling of being totally recharged when fall begins. And on Labor Day weekend, the bridge between the two seasons, I get the best of both worlds: a last chance to bask in lazy summer, and a small taste of the wildly busy fall social scene that lies in store.

In our Sag Harbor community, Labor Day weekend means morning-to-night socializing as the summer crowd says its goodbyes. The activities begin first thing on Saturday morning, when crowds congregate for the end-of-season basketball tournament. One of the village residents supplies the T-shirts, and local boys and girls supply the energy. The games bring out mobs of sports enthusiasts, with or without children of their own, to cheer on the players.

Orzo Paella with shrimp, mussels, clams, and sausage

PERSONALIZED PAINTED GLASSWARE

TIME REQUIRED: 15 to 20 minutes per piece (depending on how elaborate you get, and the number and of colors and pieces)

MATERIALS

clean, sturdy glassware

brushes of varying thickness made for watercolor (known as scrollers or liner brushes; they do nice lines and give you more control)

glass cleaner

Liquitex Glossies paint or any craft paint made for glassware (check the label)

damp cloth or paper towels (in case of mistakes)

lazy Susan or small, portable ceramic wheel (from craft shop; to help get even lines)

NOTE: You must keep all painted areas away from any area that will come in contact with food or beverages. To be extra safe, we painted only the underside of the plates and well below the lip line on the glasses. Remember to work in a well-ventilated space.

1 Select glassware, clear or colored. Clean the surfaces well.

2 Before you begin, spend a few moments planning out the design. These glasses and plates were done freehand, but if you prefer, you can find stencils at a craft or art supply store.

The aroma of hot dogs and hamburgers starts wafting over the neighborhood. In our beach community, they've closed off a street for the block party. You just have to follow your nose to find it in full swing, with grills going and everybody eating their fill, with kids running races, playing games, and winning medals. Mingling in the crowd is like being at a class reunion. Every few steps you take, you run into an old friend.

Every year, some group of brave young girls spends days putting together a dance routine for the party. Their performance kicks off the night's activity. The music's great, the dancing is sassy, and the crowd gets into the spirit with hoots and whistles. Then the DJ turns the music up loud and opens the floor to anyone who's in the mood to rock to the beat. The night is charged with the electricity of energetic dancers, young and old. As the evening draws to a close, I think how lucky we city dwellers are to be part of this small-town ritual.

Because so many people schedule last-fling Labor Day barbecues for Sunday and Monday afternoon, we decided to try something a little different. I wanted to give my guests a chance to really indulge in the sleepy pace of their seaside summers before they were thrust back into city life. And I realized that a relaxed Sunday evening dinner party on the beach would be the way to do it.

3 Paint your design using Liquitex Glossies, which are latex paints meant specifically for glassware, or choose any paint that is made to be used on glass or nonporous surfaces and can be baked.

4 Put your plate or glass in the center of the lazy Susan or wheel. Load your brush with paint, touch it to the glass and, holding your hand steady, spin the wheel several times. Don't worry about making perfect lines. Part of the charm of handmade work is that each piece has its unique imperfections.

5 If you make a mistake and the paint is still wet, simply wipe it off with water and start over.

6 Let the paint dry overnight. Then place the items in a cold oven. Heat the oven to 325 degrees and bake the glassware for 30 to 45 minutes.

7 Turn off the oven and let it cool completely before removing glassware.

NOTE: To keep your plates or glasses looking good for a long time, gently hand-wash them in warm, soapy water and rinse well.

Nobody would be watching the clock to figure out when to rush off to the next event or when to pack the car and head back to the city in time to beat the crowds. A late supper would give my beach-loving friends a full day of swimming and sunning, as well as plenty of time to relax and dress for the evening.

There's something about the word "supper" that says laid-back, languid, nothing rushed. It's the end of the day, and you're ready to relax and enjoy yourself. A supper party means deep conversation: You're going to talk well into the night. And if you're dining on the beach, there's romance, too, and the peacefulness that always comes when you're near water. This was everybody's last opportunity to slip into their sarongs, long gauzy gowns, or caftans. The men got a chance to don their most flamboyant shirts and pastel jackets. And I put on something silky and prepared a table and meal for a lazy night.

When we renovated our greenhouse, a slatted wooden workbench was left inside, which we salvaged and made into a long, rustic-style dining table that I happen to love. This table is too large for the house, but it's perfect to carry down to the beach for those indoor-outdoor dinners.

I wanted my table to look especially pretty in the seaside setting. I put out small vases of pink, orange, and lavender country flowers that picked up on the colors in the sunset. I scattered starfish among the place settings, lit some candles in hurricane candle holders, and set out a new set of glass dinnerware that I'd hand-painted with a flowing design to add a sense of movement to the table.

One day at the restaurant I was chatting with a customer who mentioned that she had just spent a small fortune in Venice on a set of eight wine goblets. She had them painted with tiny floral designs to match an exquisitely embroidered set of napkins. That conversation inspired me to try my hand at painting glassware. I discovered that with even a simple design, you can transform plain, inexpensive stemware and plates into something that makes your table setting unique. And since glassware is affordable and easy to find, it's a great "canvas" for your artwork. You can paint plates and stemware to match place mats or napkins or a distinctive serving piece, or let your imagination lead the way.

In painting my dinnerware, I wasn't trying to match a particular item, just the colors of sky and sea and sun. My palette was inspired by a tiny, painted pitcher I had found that reminded me of being by the water; my pattern—free-form swirls and waves—came from the ocean and beach grass and seashells. I painted stemware and salad plates and, using complementary shades, a set of dinner plates to use as chargers. When I placed the smaller plates on top of the larger ones, the colors showed through and made a beautiful painting. I served the salad on the glass plates and the main course on the chargers. With their periwinkle borders against the saffron yellow of the paella that I served, the dinner plates reflected the dusk blue sky with its last rays of sun.

I used to make paella, a zesty and flavorful Spanish specialty, when I threw parties back in my modeling days. A mixture of chicken and various types of seafood in the shell mixed with tomatoes and other vegetables and heaped on a fragrant mound of grain, it's an easy dish to throw together for several people, and it makes a memorable party entrée. Every now and then I run into an old friend who will nostalgically recall my paella parties.

Though paella is usually made with rice, I thought I'd give it a little twist by substituting orzo, an almond-shaped pasta that's used in Mediterranean cuisine. I served it in my paellera—a large, shallow pot designed to sit on an outdoor fire and let the rice cook evenly while the shells slowly open. Along with bread salad and pitchers of fruit-filled sangria, this dish made a beautiful, satisfying, and festive meal.

A Labor Day Weekend Dinner Party for Ten

Farmstand Herb
Bread Salad

Orzo Paella

Individual Crème Brûlées
with Brandied Peaches

Sangria

*Hurricane lamps give off
the perfect amount of light
as the sun goes down.*

FARMSTAND HERB BREAD SALAD

SERVES 10

12 ounces country-style Italian bread, cut into 1-inch cubes (about 8 cups)

¾ cup extra virgin olive oil

¼ cup balsamic vinegar

4 cloves garlic, mashed

½ cup fresh basil leaves, or
1 heaping tablespoon dried basil

1 tablespoon fresh thyme leaves, or
1 teaspoon dried thyme

1 tablespoon fresh oregano leaves, or
1 teaspoon dried oregano

Salt and freshly ground black pepper to taste

6 vine-ripened tomatoes, cut in large chunks

2 medium zucchini, cut in ¼-inch rounds

1 large roasted yellow bell pepper,
coarsely chopped

¼ cup capers, drained

⅓ cup kalamata olives, pitted, for garnish

Preheat the oven to 350 degrees. Spread the bread cubes on a baking sheet and toast until golden brown, about 10 minutes. Set aside to cool. In a blender or food processor combine the olive oil, vinegar, garlic, basil, thyme, oregano, salt, and pepper. Mix until the herbs are chopped and the mixture is well combined.

In a large salad bowl, combine the bread cubes, tomatoes, zucchini, bell pepper, and capers. Pour the dressing over the salad and toss until combined. Let the salad stand at room temperature 30 minutes before serving. Garnish with kalamata olives.

ORZO PAELLA

SERVES 10

3 quarts water

1½ pounds uncooked orzo pasta

½ teaspoon crumbled saffron threads

2 tablespoons olive oil

8 ounces spicy smoked turkey sausage, sliced into ½-inch rounds

2 cups coarsely chopped red bell pepper

1½ cups chopped onions

2 cloves garlic, minced

2 cups fresh or frozen corn kernels

1½ cups fresh or frozen peas

¼ cup dry white wine

1½ teaspoons dried oregano

1 teaspoon hot paprika

½ teaspoon freshly ground black pepper

2 dozen uncooked medium-sized littleneck clams, well scrubbed

1 pound uncooked mussels, well scrubbed

1 pound uncooked shrimp, shelled and deveined

¾ cup chopped fresh parsley, divided

In a large pot, bring the water to a boil; add the orzo and saffron. Cook just until tender, about 7 to 8 minutes. Drain and set aside.

In a large pot or dutch oven, heat 1 tablespoon of the olive oil. Add the sliced sausage and cook over medium heat 3 to 4 minutes, stirring occasionally. Remove the sausage from the pan with a slotted spoon and set aside. Add the remaining tablespoon of olive oil to the pot with the bell pepper, onions, and garlic, and cook 3 minutes, until the onions begin to soften. Stir in the corn, peas, wine, oregano, paprika, and black pepper. Increase the heat to medium-high, add the clams, and cook covered, 5 minutes. Stir in the mussels and shrimp. Cook, covered, until the clam and mussel shells open and the shrimp are cooked through, approximately 6 to 7 minutes. Discard any clams and mussels that do not open. Return the sausage to the pot; stir in orzo and ½ cup of the parsley, tossing until all the ingredients are well combined.

Transfer the paella to a large platter and sprinkle with the remaining parsley. Serve immediately or cool to room temperature before serving.

INDIVIDUAL CRÈME BRÛLÉES WITH BRANDIED PEACHES

SERVES 10

3 cups heavy cream
1 tablespoon vanilla extract
8 large egg yolks
½ cup granulated sugar
¼ teaspoon salt
½ cup brown sugar
Brandied Peaches (recipe follows)

Heat oven to 300 degrees. Heat the cream and vanilla in a double boiler over low heat until hot but not boiling. In a medium bowl, whisk the egg yolks, sugar, and salt until blended. Gradually whisk in 1 cup of the hot cream. Pour the yolk mixture back into the saucepan. Cook over low heat, stirring constantly, until the mixture thickens and coats the back of a spoon, about 5 minutes. (Do not boil.) Pour into 10 ramekins or custard cups.

Place the ramekins in a large shallow roasting pan and place in the oven. Pour hot water into the pan until it is halfway up the sides of the ramekins. Bake 30 minutes, or until the custards are set but still jiggly in the center. Remove from the water bath to a wire rack to cool to room temperature. Cover each with plastic wrap and refrigerate up to 24 hours.

To serve, preheat the broiler. Remove the plastic wrap and gently blot any liquid on the top of each ramekin. Press the brown sugar through a sieve and sprinkle evenly over the top of each ramekin to cover. Place two ramekins at a time on a baking sheet. Broil, about 4 inches from the heat, until the sugar melts, watching carefully to prevent burning. Serve with the Brandied Peaches.

BRANDIED PEACHES

4 ripe peaches
3 tablespoons triple sec
1 tablespoon brandy
1 tablespoon sugar

Bring a small pot of water to a boil. Add the peaches and simmer 1 minute. Run under cold water until cool; peel and pit the peaches, then slice into a sealable food storage bag. Add the triple sec, brandy, and sugar. Seal the bag; refrigerate and let marinate 1 to 2 hours before serving.

We brought a slatted wooden workbench that we had made into a long, rustic-style dining table out to the beach to help create the perfect setting for a relaxing dinner party.

SANGRIA

This is a great summer cooler. Use a large clear glass and be sure to put some fruit in each serving. Don't be surprised if it gets eaten up.   YIELDS 12 CUPS

6 cups red wine (rosé, burgundy, Spanish)

6 cups sparkling cider

¾ cup triple sec

¾ cup brandy

Juice of 1 lime, 1 lemon, and 1 orange

Sugar or sugar syrup to taste

Thinly sliced oranges, lemons, and limes for garnish

In a large pitcher, combine the wine, cider, triple sec, brandy, and fruit juices. Stir and add the sugar. Add ice and the thinly sliced oranges, lemons, and limes.

A BID WHIST CARD PARTY

By the end of September, our beach days feel as if they're long behind us, and we're eager to get back in touch with city friends. It's time for some casual, grown-up fun—and to me, that means card parties.

Card parties were all the rage when I was a child. My mother played fairly often with her brothers and their wives, and I remember those evenings and the rituals attached to them very well. First, everyone would help bring out the card table and the folding chairs. Then, the packs of cards would be unwrapped and shuffled three times, and the hands would be dealt.

While the grown-ups played, we kids would watch television. During breaks, they'd socialize over adult beverages and snacks that didn't seem particularly child-friendly. In fact, the whole evening didn't seem particularly child-friendly. There was plenty of laughter, but the jokes went way over our heads.

Today, many of my friends have taken up card playing, and the big game now seems to be bid whist—especially in the African-American community. In fact, bid whist has become so popular that there are even national tournaments. My husband, like most of our friends who play, took up the game during his campus days. According to my good buddy Janice Lythcott, when you ask someone if they play bid whist, the standard reply is, "Sure. I went to college!" The college connection made the idea of having a bid whist party in late September seem even more right, since this is the time of year when students are heading back to school.

Bid whist became the college game of choice for a very good reason: It's a way to have a lot of fun without spending much money. Dan claims that another attraction of bid whist lies in the fact that it's not just about cards. It's also about bravado, illusion, and "kicking butt." If you're winning—or you want

A bid whist card party is my idea of grown-up fun, whether you're hosting or playing.

CARD PARTY TIPS

Count on three or four tables of four. Rent or borrow bridge tables and folding chairs. It doesn't matter if they all match, but you may want to throw matching cloths over all of them.

Say "This is the place" by leaving luminaries outside. Make them by placing a candle in a votive in an open paper bag filled with sand or in a tin can that you've poked holes in.

Do a quick check of the lavatory before any party. Make sure you have guest towels on the rack, a fresh bar of soap, a box of tissues, and a full roll of toilet tissue.

Make sure to keep a number of liquors on hand—everything from rum and Coke (pictured) to scotch and brandy.

your opponents to think you're winning— you take every opportunity to brag. Of course, if you use the language of bid whist, nobody outside your circle is likely to understand what you're bragging about (and that's what makes the game even more fun). For example, to say you're "going to Boston" means you're winning big; a Boston is when a player wins all thirteen "books" (play the game and you'll find out what that means!). When you want to convey the impression that you're getting the upper hand, you might gleefully announce that you're in Hartford—in other words, on your way to Boston. If you want to intimidate your opponents with your great card, you don't just drop it on the table. You might wave it through the air as if you were Leonard Bernstein conducting a symphony, and then slam it down. Or you might get up, take a step or two away from the table, then spin around and return with your card held up high in triumph.

As the host, one of your jobs is to make sure that everybody knows the house rules; the rules of the game vary depending on whose home it's being played in. And, since bid whist is played by partners who have to know how to read between each other's lines (is your partner bluffing or trying to tell you something about his hand?), I always think about who will play well with whom before I invite people. In fact, you don't even have to play the game to throw a great bid whist party. As a spectator, you just have to remember a few simple rules—basically, don't do anything to give away what you know about a player's hand. This game is fun, but it's deadly serious, too. To brush up on bid whist rules and etiquette, you might want to pick up Angel Beck's book *How to Play Bid Whist.*

Even though playing bid whist takes quite a bit of concentration, nobody lets that stop them from yelling and screaming across the table. Any card party—it doesn't have to be bid whist—is an excuse for a down-and-dirty evening. It's time for good friends to hang out, tell lies on each other, make big jokes at each other's expense, and tell nasty stories about each other's exes.

My husband is the bid whist fan in our family. So for my bid whist party, I wanted to create an atmosphere where people wouldn't be afraid to light up cigars at some point during the evening. I also wanted to give the party a theme. I like bringing people into an environment and giving them an experience.

So, to evoke an old-fashioned, back-room, gambling kind of feel, I decided to bring out the brown beverages (Dan jokes that what qualifies as a mixed drink for this kind of event is a glass of Scotch with a couple of ice cubes in it). I always serve something for people to eat while they're drinking, but food was not the focus of that evening.

You can make it very easy on yourself by keeping the menu light and easy. Along with the dark green spinach dip, spiced mixed nuts, and curried popcorn, I put out some bar snacks I had in the house. Die-hard card players prefer snacks that are not messy, which is a good idea. Be sure to supply lots of large napkins. If your preference is for more elaborate snacks, they should be served away from the game tables, where players feel free to indulge and clean up before returning to the table.

A Bid Whist Card Party for Eight

Basic Brown Bar

—

Spiced Mixed Nuts

—

Curried Popcorn

—

Spinach Dip

—

Potato chips and pretzels

Decanters give a touch of elegance to the basic brown beverage bar.

BASIC BROWN BAR

BROWN BEVERAGES	MIXERS
Rum	Club soda
Scotch	Tonic
Bourbon	Ginger ale
Whisky	Cola
Brandy	Bitters
Cognac	Plenty of ice
GARNISHES	
Lemons	
Limes	

This basic bar can be set up on a sideboard, a kitchen counter, or a coffee table. Look around your house. I have a chopping block that is actually a cart on four wheels with a handle, with an additional lower shelf for more usage space. The great thing here is it's mobile. Guest should help themselves. Be sure to have tumblers (6- to 10-ounce glasses), and what we in the restaurant business call highball glasses. These are usually 8 to 12 ounces. Both should be sturdy glasses. Don't forget to supply coasters.

SPICED MIXED NUTS

Spiced nuts can be made ahead and stored in an airtight container or kept in the freezer.   YIELDS 8 CUPS

½ cup (1 stick) butter
2 teaspoons salt
2 teaspoons chili powder
2 teaspoons cayenne pepper
1 teaspoon ground cumin
2 cups cashews
2 cups pecan halves
2 cups peanuts
2 cups walnut halves

Preheat the oven to 350 degrees. In a large skillet, melt the butter. Add the salt, chili powder, cayenne, and cumin. Add the nuts and toss to coat. Spread the nuts out on a baking sheet and bake until lightly browned, about 10 minutes.

CURRIED POPCORN

YIELDS 6 QUARTS

1 cup popcorn kernels

2 tablespoons mild curry powder

2 teaspoons Creole seasoning

4 tablespoons melted butter

Pop the popcorn according to package directions. Place the popped corn in a large brown paper bag. Add the curry powder, Creole seasoning, and butter. Shake to coat well.

SPINACH DIP

YIELDS 4–5 CUPS

1 large clove garlic

½ cup chopped scallions (white portion only)

One 10-ounce package frozen chopped spinach, thawed and drained well

1 cup sour cream

½ to 1 cup mayonnaise

1 teaspoon chopped fresh thyme leaves or ½ teaspoon dried thyme leaves

1 teaspoon Worcestershire sauce

1 dash Tabasco sauce or more to taste

½ teaspoon salt

¼ teaspoon freshly ground white pepper

1 round loaf crusty bread (country white, pumpernickel, etc.)

Paprika

In a blender or food processor, finely mince the garlic and scallions. Add the remaining ingredients except the bread and paprika and blend until smooth. Taste and adjust the seasonings. Refrigerate for up to 2 days. Just before serving, make a bread bowl: Cut about an inch off the top of the round loaf of bread and save it for a lid. Remove the bread from the center, hollowing out the loaf. Stir the dip well and place in the bread bowl. Sprinkle lightly with paprika. Serve the removed bread chunks along with crudités for dipping.

OCTOBER

AN AT-HOME WINE TASTING WITH HORS D'OEUVRES

October is a glorious month in the Northeast. Nature puts on her spectacular fall foliage show, and as the leaves turn from green to gold to ruby, they give a final signal that it's time to get the coats and gloves out of storage. Then, just as we're all ready to bundle up, Indian summer brings balmy days of exquisitely clear sunlight, throwing the colors of the leaves into sharp relief against the radiantly blue sky.

We watch the last of the big boats docked in the marina outside our Sag Harbor restaurant sail south for balmier waters. Then Dan and I supervise the closing of the restaurant for the season and steal some time for a much-needed rest of our own in anticipation of the hectic days ahead.

At the tasting, each of these delectable
hors d'oeuvres accompanies a specific wine.

Fall in New York City brings an endless stream of events—Broadway shows, museum openings, fund-raisers. But while there's always somewhere to go and something to do, there are not many opportunities to socialize at home with friends during that long stretch between Labor Day and Thanksgiving. People need reasons to get together. So I thought about what makes this time of year special—it's harvest time, and the prettiest month to visit wineries—and came up with the idea of an at-home wine-tasting party.

Because I'm in the restaurant business, I get invited to quite a few wine tastings. These are great opportunities to explore new wines and taste dishes prepared by top-notch chefs, and one special wine-tasting trip that started in Paris and headed south through France's wine region is firmly instilled in my memory. But many of the big, formal wine tastings are terribly stuffy and intimidating events—not what I had in mind for my party. I wanted to introduce some favorite people to wines that I particularly like, and to use that as an excuse for an evening get-together. As for all the rules that go along with a formal wine tasting, I planned only to follow the ones that are important to the *tasting*.

Wine tasting is a serious ritual, but there's no need for anyone to feel intimidated if you remember what it's really supposed to be about: sampling good wines and having fun pairing them with foods. If you've never been to a tasting, you'll discover that some unique flavors and aromas come from particular pairings. In fact, I think that one of the reasons wine keeps growing in popularity in this country is because people are developing more sophisticated tastes in food, and along with that sophistication comes a greater appreciation of how certain wines can make for an even more interesting taste sensation.

I decided to invite friends with varying levels of wine experience to a relaxed, early Sunday evening party. I sent out invitations that let everybody know the first principles for this type of event: no smoking, heavy perfumes, or strong aftershaves. All of these conflict with the aromas and scents of wines and foods. (For the same reason, I avoid using scented candles.)

I planned a series of hors d'oeuvres, each intended to lend itself to a particular wine I had selected. Serving a variety of hors d'oeuvres, with a little time for socializing between one and the next, lets your guests savor each pairing, and keeps the pace of drinking slow—after all, the whole point of the tasting is to indulge the senses, not to get intoxicated.

As the host, it's up to you to select the wine for each dish. But if you're not on secure ground in making your choices, don't hesitate to ask for help from a good wine merchant. The employees will be more than happy to share their knowledge with you. Just be sure to pick a few wines you're familiar with, and to let them know what your budget is. It's also a very good idea to bring in your menu or recipes.

Though you'll be providing the wines that you want people to taste, I think it's a nice idea to ask your most wine-savvy guest ahead of time if he or she would like to pair a wine with one of the dishes you've planned. I always make sure to invite someone who's particularly knowledgeable about wines. I let them bring a bottle of the wine they've picked for the pairing, and then encourage them to introduce it and get the discussion going. That way, I can be a guest at my own party.

Every wine tasting starts off with the lightest variety and gradually builds to the most intense. I like to serve both reds and whites, with two bottles of wine in each category (two Chardonnays, for example) to compare and contrast. I might start with a light and sparkling Blanc de Blanc, progress to heavier whites, move on to the less intense reds, and finish with a full-bodied Merlot.

The hors d'oeuvres intensify in richness, too. You can begin with a morsel (I decided on an elegant rice cake topped with caviar, but salmon would be fine), then proceed to hors d'oeuvres made with fish and chicken, both of which are appropriate with white wines (my menu progressed from spicy fish croquettes to a chicken liver pâté with chutney, served on curried toast). The last hors d'oeuvre, to go with the Merlot, is a rich barbecued pork tenderloin on sweet potato pancakes.

I prepare the hors d'oeuvres up to a point before the party, getting everything ready and waiting to slip into a skillet or pop in the oven on baking sheets. Then I finish them to order at the last moment so that the flavors will be really fresh. Doing it this way keeps me a little more occupied than I would have been had I kept the hors d'oeuvres warm in chafing dishes, but that's fine when you're trying to pace the drinking and prolong the fun.

HOW TO TASTE WINE

1 Look at the color of the wine. Hold the glass at the stem, not the bowl, so you won't get fingerprints on the glass and cloud your view, and so the warmth of your hand doesn't affect the taste of the wine.

Color is affected by the type of grape, the processing of the wine, and how old the wine is. Generally, white wines range from yellow-green, to straw, to gold, to light brown; reds range from purple, to ruby, to brick, to light deep brown. As they age, whites grow more intensely colored and reds lose color. In addition to color, note whether the wine is clear or cloudy.

2 Check the bouquet—how the wine smells. Without lifting the glass from the table, swirl it to get some oxygen into it, then pick up the glass and tilt it against your face. Move the glass away and think how you would describe the smell. Is it flowery, smoky, fruity, yeasty, earthy? Do you detect the scent of herbs, veg-etables or grass, tobacco or coffee? Certain smells indicate problems with the wine. If the wine smells like vinegar, it has turned to acid. If you smell cork, the cork has disintegrated.

3 Taste the wine. Take a small sip, then purse your lips and pull in some air. Take a few seconds to swish the wine around, then either use a spittoon or swallow. You do this to allow the flavor to reach every part of your tongue, because each can register a different impression. The tip of your tongue detects sweet tastes, the side registers acid or sour tastes, and the back of your tongue senses bitter tastes.

Wine can be described as sweet or dry, crisp (acid) or soft. You can also describe its body: whether it tastes or seems heavy or light. How intense is the flavor? Does the texture feel sweet or rough? After you swallow, what is the aftertaste (or "finish")? Does the taste of the wine stay with you? What is that taste like?

Most important: Do you like it? Would you buy it? That's a good enough reason to give it your seal of approval.

The wines need some preparation, too. Reds should be opened about thirty minutes before serving so the wine can breathe. Open sparkling wines when you're ready to taste them, to preserve the bubbles. Red wines are usually served at room temperature; whites are usually served chilled. Provide everyone with two different glasses (one for white, one for red). You'll also need two pitchers on the table, one empty and one full of water. Before going on to a new taste, you should clear your glass for the next round by pouring some water into it, swirling it around, and pouring it off into the empty pitcher.

One wine-tasting rule I like to follow is the white tablecloth. With white as a background, you can see the true colors of the wines through the glass. Once you have some experience with wines, you'll know that you can expect a certain type of taste just from observing how a wine looks. (Looking at the wine is the first of three steps you'll take in tasting any wine; see box above for all three steps.) As the host, you might prefer to save your most delicate white cloth for another occasion and cover the table with something a little less precious. There will be spills!

When you go to a formal tasting, you are supposed to spit out your wine into a communal spittoon. (The point is to sample the wines without getting drunk.) Spitting takes practice and is not my favorite activity, so that's a rule I dispense with. Instead, I recommend that people take just a small sip of everything. But, for those who like to spit out their wine before going on to the next, I provide large coffee cups to serve as individual spittoons.

There's a lot of ritual involved in a true tasting. Some of this ritual is connected with the fact that different areas of the tongue register different tastes—and most of the ritual involves things your mother would never have let you do at table. To savor the wine at a tasting, you're supposed to swish it around in your mouth so it comes into contact with all the taste buds, and suck in a mouthful of air to oxygenate it. And that's after you've gotten a noseful of the wine's aroma. It's all part of the evening's entertainment!

Some people like to record their impressions of the different wines they've tasted in a special diary, so they know what they want to go back to. To help them along—or just for fun—you might want to give everyone a sheet of paper divided into columns, with headings for appearance, scent, body, and taste. Then, have each person write down their comments after every sampling and read their jottings aloud. (Sometimes I soak the labels off empty bottles so my guests can put their favorites in their notebooks.) Even if people don't fill in response sheets, you can be sure that they'll discuss the wines and tell anyone who'll listen about the one they recently tasted at such and such an event. When you throw a wine-tasting party, you have to expect people to show off.

This is definitely a gathering where you should finish by bringing out the coffee urn or the espresso machine. Have your cups and saucers, spoons and sugar ready to carry to the table, and encourage your guests to linger awhile over a hot cupful before they go on their way.

An At-Home Wine Tasting
with Hors d'Oeuvres for Twelve

Gruyère Risotto Cakes with Herbed Sour Cream and Caviar

J Brut, Jordan, Sonoma County, 1993
Domaine Carneros Reserve, Tattinger, 1992

Spicy Fish Croquettes on Cucumber Rounds

Pinot Grigio, La Colombaia, Italy, 1997
Chardonnay, Sonoma Cutrer, Russian River Valley, 1997

Chicken Pâté with Sweet Apple Chutney on Curried Toast

New Zealand, Riesling, Saint Clair, Marlborough, 1997
Pinot Blanc, Lucien Albrecht, Alsace, 1996

NOTE: I've listed some of my favorite wines to accompany these hors d'oeuvres, but you should feel free to experiment with many different brands and varieties of these wines.

Barbecued Pork Tenderloin on Sweet Potato Pancakes

Merlot, Cape Bay, South Africa, 1996
Merlot Lagaria, Italy, 1996

GRUYÈRE RISOTTO CAKES with HERBED SOUR CREAM and CAVIAR

YIELDS 36 PIECES

5 tablespoons butter

1¼ cups arborio rice

2¾ cups chicken broth, very hot, divided

2 large eggs, beaten

1 cup shredded Gruyère cheese

4 tablespoons finely minced fresh oregano or thyme

½ teaspoon salt

1 tablespoon dry bread crumbs

Vegetable oil spray

½ cup sour cream

1 ounce black caviar eggs (see Note)

Place a rack in the center of the oven. Preheat the oven to 350 degrees.

In a medium saucepan, over medium heat, melt the butter. Add the rice and stir to coat well for 1½ minutes. Add 2 cups of the hot broth to rice. Reduce the heat to maintain a steady low simmer. Cook uncovered, stirring occasionally. In about 10 minutes, when almost all of the liquid has been absorbed, add ½ cup more broth. In about 7 minutes, when the broth is absorbed, test the rice; it should be tender, but still firm. If necessary, continue cooking, adding broth gradually to keep the rice slightly wet. You may not need all of the broth. Cool for a few minutes in the saucepan.

Add the eggs, cheese, 3 tablespoons of the oregano or thyme, the salt, and bread crumbs to rice; mix well. Spray a 10-inch pie plate with oil. Pour the rice mixture into pan, spreading evenly to create a flat top. Bake 17 minutes. Cool 10 minutes.

Cut out shapes to create rice cakes with 1½ to 2-inch cookie cutters. Reshape the remaining rice mixture to form patties and continue cutting out shapes, using all of the mixture. Place the cakes on a serving platter.

Mix together the remaining 1 tablespoon of the oregano or thyme with the sour cream. Place a small dollop of herbed sour cream, then caviar, on top of each risotto cake. Serve.

NOTE: You may substitute salmon eggs for the caviar.

Gruyère Risotto Cakes with
Herbed Sour Cream and Caviar
served with sparkling wines

SPICY FISH CROQUETTES on CUCUMBER ROUNDS

YIELDS 36 PIECES

8 ounces cooked fresh or
canned salmon

8 ounces cup crabmeat

3/4 cup Creamy Mashed Potatoes
(see page 192)

1 1/2 tablespoons chopped fresh dill,
plus sprigs

1 teaspoon dry mustard

1 teaspoon Old Bay Seasoning

1/4 teaspoon cayenne pepper

1/4 teaspoon salt

Vegetable oil for frying

1 large cucumber, cut into 1/4-inch-
thick slices

Chili Mayonnaise (recipe follows)

Dill sprigs for garnish

In a large bowl, combine the salmon, crab, mashed potatoes, and seasonings. Shape into 1/2-inch round patties. In a large nonstick skillet, heat 3 tablespoons of the oil and fry the croquettes, without overcrowding, until golden brown, about 2 minutes per side. Drain on paper towels. Heat more oil as needed for the next batch. Keep warm while cooking the remaining croquettes.

On each cucumber round, spread some Chili Mayonnaise and top with a croquette. Garnish with a sprig of dill.

CHILI MAYONNAISE

YIELDS 1/2 CUP

1/2 cup mayonnaise

1 tablespoon finely chopped fresh
jalapeño pepper

Few drops Tabasco sauce

In a small bowl, mix together all the ingredients.

CHICKEN PÂTÉ with SWEET APPLE CHUTNEY on CURRIED TOAST

YIELDS 24 SLICES

½ cup (1 stick) butter
3 tablespoons minced onion
½ pound chicken livers
½ teaspoon ground allspice
½ teaspoon dry mustard
½ teaspoon salt
⅛ teaspoon cayenne pepper
½ teaspoon unflavored gelatin
2 tablespoons heavy cream
Curried Toast (recipe follows)
Sweet Apple Chutney (recipe follows)

In a medium skillet, over medium-low heat, melt the butter. Add the onion and sauté for 2 minutes. Add the chicken livers, allspice, dry mustard, salt, and cayenne. Cook the livers until brown on the outside and just cooked through, 6 to 8 minutes. Let cool slightly.

In a food processor, puree the liver mixture with the gelatin and cream until smooth. Place the puree onto a sheet of waxed paper and roll up tightly into a log about 4 × 2 inches, tucking in the edges well. Refrigerate several hours or overnight.

Cut the pâté into 24 slices. Place the pâté on top of a slice of Curried Toast and top off with Sweet Apple Chutney.

SWEET APPLE CHUTNEY

YIELDS ABOUT 1 CUP

3 medium Granny Smith green apples, peeled, cored, halved, and sliced thinly (about 4 cups)
2 tablespoons chopped onion
2 tablespoons dark brown sugar (or more to taste)
1 tablespoon grated fresh ginger
¼ teaspoon ground cinnamon
2 teaspoons vinegar

In a nonreactive 2-quart saucepan, combine all the ingredients. Simmer uncovered over very low heat, stirring occasionally, until soft, about 35 minutes. (If the apples get too dry, add a splash of water.) Remove from the heat; let cool. Chill until ready to serve. The chutney will keep in the refrigerator up to 1 month.

CURRIED TOAST

YIELDS 24 SLICES

*1 French baguette, sliced thinly
on the diagonal*
Butter, at room temperature
Curry powder

Brush the bread slices with the soft butter. Sprinkle with curry powder. Place on broil pan and broil briefly until lightly browned; be careful to keep a close watch so as not to burn.

BARBECUED PORK TENDERLOIN ON SWEET POTATO PANCAKES

YIELDS 24 SLICES

¼ cup dark brown sugar
2 teaspoons hot paprika
2 teaspoons ground allspice
2 teaspoons minced garlic
*1 teaspoon freshly ground
black pepper*
½ teaspoon salt
1 pound pork tenderloin
2 teaspoons vegetable oil
*⅓ cup B.'s Sweet Maple Barbecue
Sauce (see page 109)
or store-bought sauce*
*Sweet Potato Pancakes
(recipe follows)*

In a medium bowl, combine the brown sugar, paprika, allspice, garlic, pepper, and salt. Mix well. Pat the pork dry with paper towels and coat evenly with the dry rub mixture. Wrap tightly in a sheet of plastic wrap, place on a plate, and let marinate in the refrigerator up to 24 hours.

Place a rack in the center of the oven. Preheat the oven to 450 degrees.

Bring the pork to room temperature (about 30 minutes). In a large nonstick skillet, over medium heat, warm the oil. Brown the pork on all sides, being careful not to burn.

Transfer the pork onto a sheet of foil and place in a shallow baking pan. Place in the oven and roast until a meat thermometer inserted 2 inches into the center registers 155 degrees, about 15 minutes. Remove the pork from the oven and place on a cutting board with drainage slots. Cut the pork into 24 slices. Layer the pork onto a new sheet of foil and return to the baking pan. Drizzle with a mixture of half of the natural juices collected on the cutting board and the barbecue sauce. Bake 5 minutes longer. Place each slice of pork on top of a Sweet Potato Pancake.

SWEET POTATO PANCAKES

YIELDS 24 PANCAKES

*10 ounces sweet potatoes or yams,
peeled and shredded*

2 large eggs, beaten

2 tablespoons all-purpose flour

⅛ teaspoon ground cinnamon

⅛ teaspoon ground nutmeg

*⅛ teaspoon freshly ground
black pepper*

⅛ teaspoon salt

¼ cup vegetable oil

In a medium bowl, mix all the ingredients together, except for the oil. In a large nonstick skillet, over medium heat, warm 2 tablespoons of the oil. Drop the mixture by the rounded tablespoonful into the pan and cook the pancakes 1 to 2 minutes per side, or until crisp and lightly browned. Remove from the pan and drain on paper towels. Add more oil to the pan as needed for the next batch. Serve hot or at room temperature.

HALLOWEEN DINNER IN A CAULDRON

For weeks before Halloween, ideas float in and out of our conversations as Dana, Dan, and I try to decide on our own particular method of costume madness. Last year, I transformed myself into an ugly, green-faced witch with a bulbous nose and blackened teeth. I must have done a good job, because when I appeared in the lobby of our New York apartment building, I truly scared some of the smaller revelers. What's more, my staff didn't recognize me as I swished into the New York B. Smith's, magic broom in hand. The maître d' was about to escort me out when I greeted him by name—and he realized this was no witch, this was his boss!

Halloween parties have been an American custom for over a century. In the early days, people would decorate the outsides of their houses for the occasion; they'd make cornhusk door knockers, trim their gables with yellow chrysanthemums, and twine autumn leaves around their porch columns. I think there's a trend back to this sort of thing. When we drive around Long Island during this time of year, we see many more Halloween yard and home decorations than we saw a decade ago.

Naturally, we wouldn't miss a chance to participate. Along with huge pumpkins, we put candles and gourds out on the porch of our Sag Harbor house. Then, on Saturday morning, we get up for the much-anticipated costume parade through Sag Harbor's downtown. Practically the whole town turns out. Merchants open their doors and fill the kids' bags with treats, and prizes are given for the most creative costumes.

SAFETY TIPS FOR TRICK-OR-TREATING

■ Check with families along the route ahead of time to see if they will welcome trick-or-treaters. Provide the kids or an adult accompanying them with a map of houses, and have the houses on the route identify themselves with a porchlight, candle, or other special sign of welcome. If you live in an apartment building, post a sign-up sheet for people to indicate if they will welcome children, and during what hours.

■ Ask the families who will be giving out the treats not to distribute any edibles that aren't commercially wrapped, and tell the children not to accept or eat anything that is unwrapped.

■ If possible, incorporate a flashlight into your child's costume—Lady Liberty's torch, or a magician's wand. Alternatively, tape a spooky stencil over the flashlight beam to make a projectable design. Or you can put a flashlight in a jack-o'-lantern for that special glow.

■ Use reflective tape on costumes, shoes, trick-or-treat bags—or wherever. If children are on the roadside, drivers will spot them.

Halloween's costume parades and treats date way back to the days when Celts disguised themselves as ghouls so that evil spirits might mistake them for friends and leave them unharmed. Sometimes Celtic villagers would parade to the town limits, hoping to lead the evil spirits away, and sometimes they'd try to pacify them by giving them sweets. Ancient rituals have continued to stay alive in our modern celebrations.

The afternoon of the parade, we have a standing invitation to our next-door neighbor's home for what kids would rate as an "awesome" Halloween-themed birthday party for their youngest daughter. Though the invitation says "with or without costume," there are always more in the "with" category.

In the evening, we gather at another friend's home to bob for apples and munch on snacks meant to fortify our motley crew on the trick-or-treat route. As we pass through empty, wooded lots, the creaking twigs and rustling leaves do a great job of raising the night's spookiness factor. For me, Halloween is all about indulging in fantasy, but it has to be scary too.

After an evening of trick-or-treating, ghosts and goblins take a break to file into the kitchen, where they help themselves to my bubbling cauldrons.

When Dana was smaller, I used to invite family friends with children to spend Halloween weekend with us in Sag Harbor so the children could go trick-or-treating together. By the time we got back home, we'd have worked up quite an appetite. In anticipation of this, I would make sure I had something hearty and warming ready on the stove.

That's how my witch's cauldron tradition got started. Like the good witches of old, on Halloween weekend I cook up three cauldrons, each with its own soup or stew bubbling and ready to dip into when we return from trick-or-treating. I might make a pumpkin-apple soup, an oxtail stew, and a savory seafood chowder—foods that warm the soul and stick to the ribs.

DECORATIVE GOURDS

It's fun to carve Halloween pumpkins, but after just a few days, they start looking more saggy than scary. Instead, you could decorate gourds that will last for ages. Gourds can be painted and stained in a number of different ways, and are surprisingly versatile as decorative props. Short, squat ones make good containers, and any number of shapes can be used as vases for dried flower arrangements. I use decorated gourds as ornaments on my Kwanzaa tree, and group eight of them together, with a candle in each, to make the traditional kinara (a Kwanzaa candleholder).

This is a project kids can do, too, with your help (you prepare the gourd; they paint it).

TIME REQUIRED: 2 to 4 hours

MATERIALS:

gourds

utility saw

scraper and scrub brush to clean gourd

lightweight sandpaper

painter's tape in varying widths (we used 1- and 2-inch rolls)

any of the following: liquid shoe polish, watercolor, acrylic craft paints; permanent watercolor markers work well for decorating outsides of gourds

spray acrylic varnish or wax

1 Select gourds. You could dry them on your own (which takes 6 to 8 weeks) or purchase them already dried (see page 235).

2 Cut the gourd top, using a saw or heavy utility knife. How you cut it will depend on the shape you want to end up with—whether you plan to use it as a vase or bowl, or as a container with a lid.

3 Clean the interior of the gourd with the scraper.

4 Once it is all cleaned out, sand the inside area with a lightweight sandpaper. (Do not use this on the outside of the gourd. It will scratch the surface, making it hard to work on.)

Having three cauldrons going is kind of fun—especially when you invite people to go into the kitchen and ladle portions directly from the pots simmering on the stove. And there's always plenty for everyone, including the friends we run into along the way. You never know how many ghouls you'll end up feeding on Halloween. I put out a basket of warm breads and crackers on the counter so that people can help themselves. As for dessert, I don't have to worry about it. There's plenty of candy waiting.

Some years, when the last day of October falls on a weekday, we celebrate two Halloweens: the Saturday parade and trick-or-treating in Sag Harbor, and Halloween proper in New York. Trick-or-treating in the city tends to be an indoor affair—the kids in our apartment building travel from floor to floor—so there's not much call for cauldrons of soup. But Dan, who loves giving a jolt to the little witches, ghosts, and princesses who come knocking at our door, decorates our apartment in a suitably revolting manner. Bloody handprints, thick cob-

5 If there is any mold inside the gourd, soak it in water with a capful of bleach for 15 to 30 minutes and scrub the section with a plastic scrubber.

6 If you want to create a design of stripes and small repeating patterns, use painter's tape. Or you could do something freeform.

7 Apply liquid shoe polish and rub it in with soft cloth. For a different look, you could also apply an acrylic, watercolor, or oil-based paint over a permanent marker. Kids especially love to work in bright colors.

8 When the paint is dry, apply a spray acrylic varnish or wax polish to protect the design.

webs, and gross green mold cover the door (left slightly ajar, the better to entice the kids), and the sound of eerie music floats out

These hollowed-out decorative gourds can be a fun fall project. I use them as a centerpiece, a vase, or an ornament.

to greet visitors. Inside, the apartment looks like a place the Addams family would be proud to call home.

To appease the trick-or-treaters, we offer them their choice from a huge platter full of miniature juice boxes, which is the treat we prefer to give: The kids already have enough candy in their bags to keep them going until Christmas, and they're usually thirsty.

Later in the evening, I often go over to B. Smith's restaurant, where I put little tricks or treats—a funny little rubber bug or a small bag of candy—on the tables reserved for any groups of people I know. Halloween is a kids' holiday, but you don't have to be a kid to enjoy playing with its traditions in all sorts of little ways.

Halloween Dinner in a Cauldron for Six

Pumpkin-Apple Soup

—

Oxtail Stew

—

Savory Seafood Chowder

Old-Fashioned Halloween Pumpkin Biscuits

—

Assorted breads and crackers

Warm apple cider

Chardonnay, Estancia, Monterey County, 1997
(or any other Chardonnay)

Merlot, Kunde Estate Sonoma Valley, 1996
(or any other Merlot)

PUMPKIN-APPLE SOUP

The perfect fall soup with a hint of sweetness from the apples can be made a day ahead. Refrigerate uncovered until cold and then cover until ready to reheat and serve.
SERVES 6

2 tablespoons unsalted butter

1 onion, diced

2 large green apples, peeled, cored, and diced

1 tablespoon all-purpose flour

4 cups chicken or vegetable stock

3 cups pumpkin puree

2 tablespoons brown sugar

1 teaspoon ground cinnamon

1 teaspoon ground nutmeg

1 teaspoon ground ginger

1 cup apple juice

½ cup half-and-half

Salt and freshly ground pepper to taste

¼ cup toasted pumpkin seeds for garnish (optional)

In a large saucepan over low heat, melt the butter. Add the onion and apples, and sauté until soft. Add the flour; stir and cook 2 to 3 minutes. Gradually add the chicken or vegetable stock, whisking thoroughly. Add the pumpkin puree, brown sugar, and spices. Bring to a boil, reduce the heat, and simmer partially covered for 25 minutes. Transfer the soup to a blender or food processor and puree until smooth. Return the soup to the saucepan. Stir in the apple juice, half-and-half, salt, and pepper. Adjust spices to taste. If necessary, stir in a little more apple juice to thin the soup. Sprinkle with toasted pumpkin seeds, if desired. Serve warm.

OXTAIL STEW

SERVES 6

½ cup all-purpose flour

1 tablespoon sweet paprika

1 teaspoon salt

½ teaspoon freshly ground black pepper

6 pounds oxtail, excess fat removed and cut into pieces

¼ cup vegetable oil

3 cups beef stock

¾ cup red wine

Two 28-ounce cans plum tomatoes

1 large onion, sliced

3 ribs celery, chopped

2 cloves garlic, minced

2 bay leaves

1 tablespoon Worcestershire sauce

½ pound Red Bliss potatoes, halved

2 large carrots, peeled and cut in ½-inch rounds

¼ cup chopped fresh parsley for garnish

In a pie plate or on a piece of waxed paper, mix together the flour, paprika, salt, and pepper. Dredge the oxtail pieces in the flour mixture, shaking off excess. In a large skillet, over medium-high heat, heat the oil. Working in batches and being careful not to crowd the skillet, brown the oxtails on all sides. Transfer the oxtails to a large soup pot or dutch oven.

Add the beef stock and red wine to the pot. Drain the tomatoes, reserving 1½ cups juice. Add the juice to the pot. Bring to a boil and cook 5 minutes, removing the scum that forms on the top. Add the onions, celery, garlic, and bay leaves. Reduce the heat and simmer, partially covered, 2½ to 3 hours, until the oxtails are very tender. Remove the pot from the heat. Using a slotted spoon, transfer the oxtails and vegetables to a large bowl; set aside. Skim off the fat from the broth. Return the oxtails and vegetables to the pot. Bring to a simmer. Chop the drained tomatoes; add to the stew with the Worcestershire sauce, potatoes, and carrots. Simmer, covered, until the vegetables are tender, about 25 minutes. Season to taste with salt and pepper. Sprinkle with the parsley to serve.

SAVORY SEAFOOD CHOWDER

SERVES 6

3 tablespoons butter

1 medium onion, finely diced

½ cup finely diced celery

3 cloves garlic, finely chopped

4 cups fish stock or clam juice

1 bay leaf

1½ teaspoons dried thyme

½ cup finely diced carrots

1½ cups peeled, diced, seeded tomatoes

1½ teaspoons Old Bay Seasoning

1 pound monkfish, cut into 1½-inch chunks

½ pound scallops

½ pound fillet of bass or red snapper, cut into 1½-inch chunks

12 ounces mini bow tie pasta, cooked

Salt and freshly ground black pepper to taste

Chopped fresh parsley for garnish

In a large soup pot or saucepan, over medium heat, melt the butter. Sauté the onion, celery, and garlic until softened. Add the fish stock or clam juice, bay leaf, thyme, carrots, diced tomatoes, and Old Bay Seasoning. Bring to a boil. Reduce the heat and add the fish. Simmer partially covered about 15 minutes, until the fish is cooked through. Add the pasta and heat until the pasta ia warmed. Season with salt and pepper. Garnish with parsley.

OLD-FASHIONED HALLOWEEN PUMPKIN BISCUITS

YIELDS 12 BISCUITS

2 cups all-purpose flour

2 teaspoons baking powder

½ teaspoon baking soda

1 teaspoon salt

¼ cup (½ stick) chilled butter or shortening

½ cup pumpkin puree

½ cup buttermilk

Preheat the oven to 450 degrees. In a food processor, sift together the flour, baking powder, baking soda, and salt. Add the butter or shortening and pulse until it is the texture of coarse meal. Add the pumpkin and buttermilk to the flour mixture. Process until the dough is soft and easy to handle. Turn onto a lightly floured work surface. Knead the dough gently until smooth. Roll out to ½-inch thickness, and cut with a biscuit cutter. Place the biscuits on a lightly greased baking sheet. Bake 10 to 12 minutes, or until lightly browned.

NOVEMBER

THANKSGIVING DINNER

I've always loved this time of the year. It's crisp and bright and sunny, and out in the country, you can still see a few pumpkins in the fields. There's a harvesty feeling in the air that wakes up all of your senses. To me, that feeling means Thanksgiving.

Thanksgiving was my mother's holiday. Just as the whole family would converge on my aunt and uncle's house for other holidays, on Thanksgiving, they all gathered around our table. Every year, I'd insist on staying up late the night before to help my mother make her elaborate holiday preparations. How could I go to bed when there were so many exciting things to do, from washing the good china, polishing the silver, and pressing the linens to cutting, chopping, and stirring ingredients for all the dishes?

While everyone has a favorite way of preparing their Thanksgiving bird, I like to go with a jerked roast turkey. Jerk sauce gives the turkey just the right amount of extra flavor

In my house when I was growing up, everything was a heightened experience during Thanksgiving. It was a time to bring out the good china, the silver, the coffee urn (we never had fresh-brewed coffee unless we had company), and all of these things had to be sparkling. So the anticipation started days in advance. Then, the day before Thanksgiving, the cooking began, and the house started filling up with all those wonderful aromas.

Like any holiday, Thanksgiving is not just about the foods that we eat. It's also about the rituals we perform. While those rituals might include lighting the candles on Hanukkah or wrapping gifts at Christmas, on Thanksgiving—our harvest celebration—they revolve around planning and preparing a feast.

Even today, just as in my mother's time, the preparation starts early. You have to buy the turkey early, whether you're putting in an order for a fresh one or buying a frozen turkey before they're all gone. You make your cranberry sauce and cornbread in advance (you don't want the bread to be so fresh that it's crumbly). You scan your shelves, making sure you have everything you need so you don't have to run out at the last moment. You think about nothing but food for a week. And then the day comes and you eat. And eat.

New York City has its own Thanksgiving ritual: the Macy's Thanksgiving Day Parade. If we're in Manhattan the evening before, Dan and Dana and I sometimes take a stroll to the Upper West Side to watch the huge balloons being readied for the parade. There's a festive air as spectators jostle through the crowded streets, children on their shoulders, eager to catch a glimpse of the balloons slowly inflating. The next morning, we always watch the parade, whether we're spectators on the street (which has its own excitement), catch it on television, or attend one of the parties hosted by friends whose apartments overlook the parade route.

If we're not in the city, we generally have a homemade Thanksgiving with friends in Sag Harbor. Though I enjoy being creative about my menus, I don't tamper too much with the classic Thanksgiving feast. I just make a few little adjustments here and there.

I like the idea of making a traditional Thanksgiving meal because this is the one holiday we have that cuts across differences of religion and ethnicity. Around the country, everybody celebrates Thanksgiving—and almost always with turkey.

Just as turkey means Thanksgiving, so do cranberry sauce, gravy, creamy mashed potatoes, candied yams, and pumpkin pie. It just wouldn't be Thanksgiving without them. But of

To celebrate the harvest season, I've decorated the table with autumn-colored candles and russet napkins. My centerpiece is made of wheat (most florists sell a version of this) surrounded by fruits and nuts on a piece of Kuba cloth.

course, there's nothing wrong with a little updating. Standard cranberry sauce is fine, but one year I decided to try something new. I added persimmons and cloves to the sauce, and everybody liked it. Next year, I'll try something else! I also thought I'd try an old-fashioned variation on the classic pumpkin pie: My mother used to make pies in a skillet; I did the same, adding apples.

Turkey is the culinary equivalent of the little black dress—it's amazingly versatile, and easy to transform into something a little spicy. It goes well with almost every kind of condiment, sauce, and side dish, and it can be prepared in any number of ways. Some of my friends in the Southwest cook their bird by deep-frying it outdoors in a kettle. Others smoke it.

My family prefers jerk-seasoned turkey, which goes nicely with a jalapeño cornbread dressing—the yellow color of the cornbread looks especially pretty. I had my first taste of jerk seasoning in Jamaica, and remembered it when I was trying to do something different with turkey for a party. I marinated the turkey in the sauce to make it moist and tender and very tasty. Since I didn't want a really spicy roast, just something well seasoned, I rubbed the jerk sauce off the turkey before covering it with butter and putting it in the oven. That turkey was a huge success, so I put it on the restaurant menu. Since I think of the restaurant as my dining room away from home, I frequently have the same dishes in both places. Jerked roast turkey is now a Thanksgiving Day staple at both.

I never skimp on the items that I'm using in my cooking, especially at Thanksgiving. I use lots of butter and cream in the mashed potatoes. I make the candied yams extrasweet. I'll even prepare extra turkey parts—especially legs—to accommodate the preferences of my guests. Everything is a little over the top, because this is a holiday for feasting. Whereas I might be watching all of our weights on any other day, Thanksgiving is an occasion to overdo it.

I always make enough food to have leftovers, and sometimes I send guests off with little packages of leftover turkey or cornbread. Many times, I'll invite people to Thanksgiving who don't much like to cook, or who live alone and don't see the point in cooking. So when they get home and start to feel a little hungry again, they can open up their package and have a small, late-night Thanksgiving snack.

Because Thanksgiving is such a seasonal holiday, I like to decorate my table in a way that says harvest time. This year, I used autumn-colored candles and russet napkins, and made a centerpiece of wheat, which I surrounded with fruits and nuts and placed on a piece of Kuba cloth. I always try to use ethnic accents in my decoration: Kuba cloth is made in what was once the kingdom of Kuba (now in Zaire). It seemed perfect for this table, because it's made from earthy-toned raffia.

I set all the food out on a side buffet, just as my mother used to do whenever we had our holiday meals. With the candlelight adding an extra hint of yellow, our feast had in it all the colors of the fall season.

Thanksgiving Dinner for Eight

Jerked Roast Turkey

Cornbread-Jalapeño Dressing

Pan Gravy

Cranberry-Persimmon Sauce

Creamy Mashed Potatoes

Candied Yams

Winter Greens

Skillet Pumpkin-Apple Pie
with Vanilla Ice Cream

Chardonnay, Edna Valley, San Luis Obispo, 1997
(or any other Chardonnay)

White zinfandel, Deloach, Sonoma, 1997
(or any other zinfandel)

Pinot Noir, Yarra Ridge Valley, 1998
(or any other Pinot Noir)

For Thanksgiving I like to set up a buffet table that includes my personal variations on all of the holiday favorites: Jerked Roast Turkey, Candied Yams, Cornbread-Jalapeño Dressing, Winter Greens, Creamy Mashed Potatoes, and Cranberry-Persimmon Sauce.

JERKED ROAST TURKEY

SERVES 8

One 10- to 12-pound turkey

2 cups jerk sauce (store-bought—
Vernon's, Walker's Wood, etc.)

1 cup (2 sticks) butter, melted

Cornbread-Jalapeño Dressing
(recipe follows)

3 medium onions

3 medium stalks celery

5 sprigs parsley

Coarse salt and freshly ground
black pepper to taste

Remove the giblets from the turkey. Rinse the turkey inside and out with cold water. Blot dry with paper towels. Rub the jerk sauce evenly over and inside of the turkey. Place the turkey breast side down inside a 2-gallon, heavy-duty sealable plastic bag. Squeeze out as much air as possible and seal the bag. Refrigerate and marinate for 48 hours, turning occasionally.

Position the oven rack near the bottom of the oven. Preheat the oven to 350 degrees. Remove the turkey from the plastic bag. Wipe off the jerk sauce and pat dry. Rub the turkey with ¼ cup of the butter and sprinkle with salt and pepper. Stuff the turkey with the dressing or onions and celery cut into large pieces. Place the parsley inside the cavity of the turkey. Tie the legs together with kitchen string and set the turkey breast side up on a rack in a large roasting pan at least 2 inches deep. Lower the oven temperature to 325 degrees. Roast the turkey until a meat thermometer registers 180 degrees in breast meat or 185 degrees in thigh meat, approximately 3½ to 4 hours. Brush the turkey with the remaining butter, basting occasionally. When the turkey skin is golden brown, cover with foil over the breast to prevent overbrowning. Remove the turkey to a warm platter and cover loosely with a towel. Let rest 30 to 40 minutes before carving.

CORNBREAD-JALAPEÑO DRESSING

YIELDS 9–10 CUPS

*6 to 8 cups cornbread cubes
(see recipe for cornbread on page 110)*

1 cup (2 sticks) butter

2 cups chopped onions

*2 cups chopped celery
(including some leaves)*

½ cup finely chopped jalapeño peppers

2 teaspoons ground sage

2 teaspoons dried thyme leaves

2 teaspoons poultry seasoning

*Salt and freshly ground black pepper
to taste*

2 eggs, slightly beaten

1½ cups turkey or chicken stock

Preheat the oven to 350 degrees. In a large bowl, place the cornbread and set aside. In a large skillet, over medium heat, melt the butter. Add the onions, celery, and jalapeño peppers. Sauté until tender. Do not brown. Remove from heat. Stir in the sage, thyme, poultry seasoning, salt, and pepper. Add to the cornbread. Stir in the eggs. Add the turkey or chicken stock, ½ cup at a time, until the mixture is moist but not wet. Taste and adjust seasoning. Spoon dressing into a large buttered baking dish. Cover and bake 45 to 50 minutes, until the dressing is browned, or stuff the turkey with the dressing and bake as directed.

PAN GRAVY

YIELDS 3 CUPS

*3 cups combined pan drippings
and turkey or chicken stock*

¼ cup all-purpose flour

½ cup water

*Cooked chopped turkey giblets
(optional)*

*Coarse salt and freshly ground
black pepper to taste*

Using the drippings from the roasting pan, skim off all but 4 tablespoons of the fat in the pan. Place the pan over high heat. Add the turkey or chicken stock and bring to a boil, scraping the bottom to loosen browned bits. Reduce the heat. Mix the flour and water together. Whisk into the gravy. Blend well; add the giblets if desired, and simmer 5 minutes. Season with salt and pepper to taste.

CRANBERRY-PERSIMMON SAUCE

YIELDS ABOUT 2–3 CUPS

12 ounces fresh cranberries
1½ cups sugar
2 ripe persimmons, peeled and cubed
¾ cup orange juice
2 tablespoons grated orange zest
⅛ teaspoon ground cloves
1 tablespoon triple sec (optional)
½ cup chopped walnuts (optional)

In a large saucepan, combine the cranberries, sugar, persimmons, juice, and zest. Cook over medium heat, stirring occasionally, until the sugar has dissolved. Simmer about 10 minutes, until most of the berries have "popped." Stir in the ground cloves, and the triple sec and walnuts if desired. Remove from the heat and allow to cool. Refrigerate until ready to serve, at least 2 hours.

CREAMY MASHED POTATOES

SERVES 8

8 large Yukon Gold
or all-purpose potatoes
1 teaspoon salt
2 bay leaves
¾ cup (1½ sticks) unsalted butter
1 cup heavy cream, heated until warm
Salt and freshly ground black pepper to taste
¼ cup chopped fresh parsley, for garnish

Rinse and peel the potatoes, and cut them into ½-inch cubes. In a large saucepan, cover the potatoes with water. Add the salt and bay leaves and bring to a boil. Cook, covered, 20 to 30 minutes, until the potatoes are tender. Remove the bay leaves and drain well. Mash the potatoes and gradually add butter and cream until the potatoes are creamy. Season with salt and pepper and garnish with the parsley. Serve immediately.

CANDIED YAMS

This recipe can easily be modified, using less sugar. But I prefer it rich, sweet, and flavorful, especially for a holiday meal.   SERVES 8

8 medium yams or sweet potatoes

6 tablespoons butter

1½ cups dark brown sugar

1½ cups orange juice

1½ teaspoons ground nutmeg

1½ teaspoons ground cinnamon

1½ teaspoons ground ginger

Peel and cut the yams into 1-inch rounds. Boil the yams until tender, about 20 minutes. While the yams are cooking, add the remaining ingredients to a saucepan. Bring to a boil, stirring until all ingredients are melted and combined. Drain the yams and toss with the mixture. Serve immediately.

WINTER GREENS

SERVES 8

¼ cup olive oil

1 large onion, thinly sliced

3 cloves garlic, sliced

8 cups chicken or turkey stock

3 bay leaves

2 teaspoons crushed red pepper

2 teaspoons dried thyme leaves

6 pounds collard, kale, and turnip greens, cleaned and chopped

3 cups chopped smoked turkey

Salt and freshly ground black pepper to taste

In a large heavy pot, heat the olive oil. Sauté the onion and garlic until softened. Add the chicken or turkey stock, bay leaves, red pepper, and thyme. Simmer 12 minutes. Add the greens and smoked turkey. Simmer uncovered until the greens are tender. Season with salt and pepper.

SKILLET PUMPKIN-APPLE PIE with VANILLA ICE CREAM

SERVES 8

PECAN CRUNCH TOPPING

¼ cup granulated sugar

¼ cup brown sugar

¼ cup all-purpose flour

1 teaspoon ground cinnamon

⅛ teaspoon salt

⅔ cup chopped pecans

7 tablespoons unsalted butter, cut into pieces

PUMPKIN FILLING

⅓ cup granulated sugar

⅓ cup brown sugar

2 to 3 tablespoons all-purpose flour
(see Note)

1 teaspoon ground cinnamon

2 teaspoons pumpkin pie spice

1 teaspoon ground ginger

½ teaspoon salt

One 15-ounce can solid pack pumpkin

2 eggs

8 ounces sour cream

APPLE LAYER

2 tablespoons brown sugar

⅛ teaspoon ground cinnamon

1 teaspoon all-purpose flour

2 small Golden Delicious apples, peeled,
cored and sliced ⅛-inch thick

1 tablespoon unsalted butter

2 tablespoons granulated sugar

Vanilla ice cream

Cinnamon stick

Place a baking sheet on the bottom shelf of the oven. Place the oven rack for the pie on the second level up from the bottom. Preheat the oven to 425 degrees.

To make the pecan crunch topping, in a small bowl combine the sugars, flour, cinnamon, salt, and pecans. Add the butter and, using two knives or a pastry blender, cut in the butter until the mixture is crumbly. Set aside.

To make the pumpkin filling, in a small bowl stir together the sugars, flour, spices, and salt. Set aside. In a large bowl, mix the pumpkin, eggs, and sour cream until smooth. Stir in the dry ingredients.

To make the apple layer, in a large bowl, mix the brown sugar, cinnamon, and flour; toss with apples to coat evenly. In a 10- to 10½-inch iron skillet, over medium heat, melt the butter. Sprinkle the granulated sugar over the butter and cook 3 to 4 minutes, until just starting to brown; top with the apples and remove from the heat.

Pour the pumpkin filling over the apples and scatter the crunch topping over the top, leaving about a ¼-inch border of pumpkin around the edges uncovered.

Bake 10 minutes, then lower the oven temperature to 350 degrees. Bake about 40 to 45 minutes, until a knife inserted near the center comes out clean. Remove to a wire rack and cool at least 30 minutes.

To serve, spoon out of the skillet, top with a scoop of vanilla ice cream, and grate the cinnamon stick over the ice cream.

NOTE: For a softer pumpkin pie consistency, use 2 tablespoons flour. If you prefer a firmer pumpkin pie, use 3 tablespoons flour.

A DESSERT-DANCE PARTY

I don't think we dance enough these days. Dancing is one of the best ways I know to celebrate life and wake yourself up to the world. I've been an enthusiastic dancer ever since I was a kid dancing along to the Top Forty hits on Casey Kasem's weekend countdown in the basement of my parents' house. And many an evening when Dana was small, no matter how much work Dan and I had brought home or how tired we felt, the three of us would put on our favorite music and have our own private dance party.

I love to dance, and I love getting people up and dancing. Over the years, I've discovered that you don't have to do much to lure people onto the dance floor—just play a good mix of music and give them plenty of dessert. Once the rhythm gets going and the sugar from the sweets kicks in, your guests don't mind letting go of their inhibitions. That's why I love the idea of a dessert-dance party.

I first thought of this idea after a group of people came to me with a problem. They were planning a fund-raising party, but they didn't have much of a budget. Did I have any suggestions? I proposed a dessert-and-Champagne party, which I thought would be sweet, easy, and fun. It also was a huge success. Then I stole the dessert-only party idea from myself and combined it with a dance.

I decided to hold my party in November, because it's a great way to get everyone in the mood for the holidays. With this type of party, the more people you have, the merrier, and it doesn't matter if some of your guests bring a few friends—you've got plenty of desserts. But one of the great things about a dessert-dance party is that you can have one any time of the year.

With this great combination, it takes very little effort to make the night truly special. In fact, I've often thought that this would be the perfect party to throw if you happen to be someone who doesn't much like cooking—or who doesn't have time to put together a whole meal. Your party can be as lavish or as simple as you like. I wanted my party to have a very elegant feel, which is something

My dessert-dance party features a number of mouth-watering desserts, including (clockwise from top left): Triple Chocolate Torte with Pistachio Sauce and Sugared Flower Petals, Orange-Mango Triple Sec Layer Cake, White Chocolate Tiramisú, Amaretto Floating Island, and Pear Tart with Warm Brandy-Caramel Sauce.

After burning off some calories dancing, guests indulge with some White Chocolate Tiramisú.

you can do very easily and inexpensively, since the desserts themselves look so exquisite. I set up a beautiful buffet table with flowers, silver, and crystal, put out an array of tempting lavish desserts that I had prepared in advance, and added liqueurs and a coffee urn, so that my guests could drift back and forth between dancing and dessert. Then I loaded up the CD player, put on a beaded dress, and gave myself a 1960s hairdo, and I was ready.

To me, a dessert-dance party says dress-up and fantasy. When you're dressing up for this type of party, it reminds you of old books that you used to read: You feel a little special. That's what fantasy is all about—transporting yourself in time or space so that you can be whatever you want to be. You can become the queen of the ball if you want, or if you prefer, a hot flamenco dancer.

I love an excuse to dress up in any kind of costume. One Halloween at B. Smith's, I was completely taken by the Marie Antoinette outfit one of the waitresses was wearing. I couldn't wait to find a white wig and lace myself into a gown with a skirt so immense I couldn't sit down—which is what made me start thinking about a Viennese waltz party. Having lived in Vienna and spent plenty of time visiting the palaces, I knew exactly how such a party ought to look; and if you saw the movie *Amadeus,* so do you.

A dance party with a theme that calls for costumes and special music is a great way to invite friends into your fantasy and offer them something unusual. If you prefer Motown to Mozart, have a 1960s R&B night. If you wanted to, you could make it a 1950s party and do the Lindy Hop in poodle skirts, or hold a Latin salsa fiesta. Ask everyone to put on their flapper dresses and bow ties and practice doing the Charleston, or deck themselves out in vintage 1940s outfits for a night of swing dancing. Your guests could put an outfit together from what's in their closet, check out a vintage clothing shop, or go all out at the costume rental shop.

The main point of this party is to have fun. You can use a boombox and speakers or have live music, party at home or hire a hall. We've managed to squish a dance party into our space-restricted New York apartment, and a friend of ours transformed her home into dance space simply by leaving the lights off and filling the place with candles in every kind of container she could find. She even set up a centerpiece arrangement in an aquarium that had formerly housed her fish. You can have everything catered or store-bought, or make your own desserts. I always think it's fun to have the guests each bring a homemade contribution. Making desserts is one of the most fun and gratifying types of cooking, but few of us bother. A dessert party is a great excuse to get out the baking pans and whip up some luscious and rich creations.

This is the kind of party that should start mid-evening, after your guests have called it a day, had dinner, and tucked the kids into bed. Then they can put their worries behind them, slip on their party shoes, and dance the night away.

A Dessert-Dance Party for Ten

Pear Tart with
Warm Brandy-Caramel Sauce

Amaretto Floating Island

Orange-Mango Triple Sec Layer Cake
(see page 90)

Triple Chocolate Torte with Pistachio
Sauce and Sugared Flower Petals
(see page 36)

Individual White Chocolate Tiramisús
(see page 75)

Coffee	Frangelico
Bailey's Irish Cream	Grand Marnier
Sambucca	Chambord
Kahlúa	B & B

PEAR TART with WARM BRANDY-CARAMEL SAUCE

SERVES 10–12

PASTRY

¼ cup sugar

6 tablespoons unsalted butter

1 large egg yolk

1 tablespoon water

½ teaspoon vanilla extract

1¼ cups cake flour

⅓ cup ground hazelnuts

½ teaspoon ground nutmeg

Pinch salt

FILLING

½ cup apricot jam, warmed over low heat and strained

1 tablespoon apricot brandy

4 medium firm, ripe Anjou pears

1 tablespoon sugar

Warm Brandy-Caramel Sauce (recipe follows)

To make the pastry, in a bowl or a food processor, cream together the sugar, butter, egg yolk, water, and vanilla. Add the flour, hazelnuts, nutmeg, and salt; mix or process until the mixture clumps together. Spread the dough in the bottom and up the sides of a 10-inch, fluted tart pan with a removable bottom. Refrigerate, covered, 30 minutes to 1 hour. Meanwhile, preheat the oven to 425 degrees. Bake the crust 15 minutes. Remove from the oven and allow to cool. Lower the oven temperature to 375 degrees.

To make the filling, in a small bowl, stir together the warm jam and apricot brandy. Spread 2 tablespoons of the apricot glaze in a thin layer over the bottom of the hazelnut crust. Peel, core, and cut pears into halves. Cut each pear half from stem to blossom end into ⅛-inch slices. Arrange neatly overlapping pear slices in a concentric circle on the tart shell, filling in the center with uneven slices. Sprinkle with the sugar. Bake 20 to 25 minutes, until the pears are tender. While the pears are baking, reheat the jam and brandy mixture over a low heat. Remove the pears from the oven and brush the fruit with warm apricot glaze. Cool slightly before removing the sides of the tart pan. Serve warm or at room temperature with Warm Brandy-Caramel Sauce.

WARM BRANDY-CARAMEL SAUCE

½ cup heavy cream
½ cup brown sugar
¼ cup light corn syrup
2 tablespoons granulated sugar
Pinch of salt
4 tablespoons (½ stick) unsalted butter
2 tablespoons brandy

In a small nonstick saucepan, combine the cream, brown sugar, corn syrup, granulated sugar, and salt. Bring to a boil, stirring occasionally. Cook, without stirring, until the mixture reaches soft ball stage, 238 degrees on a candy thermometer. Remove from the heat and stir in the butter and brandy. Serve warm.

AMARETTO FLOATING ISLAND

SERVES 8

6 large egg whites
1 cup granulated sugar, divided
4 cups milk
6 large egg yolks
⅛ teaspoon salt
3 tablespoons Amaretto liqueur
3 tablespoons toasted chopped almonds
for garnish

In a large bowl, using an electric mixer, beat the egg whites until soft peaks form. Gradually add ½ cup of the sugar, beating until stiff peaks form. In a deep skillet or sauté pan, heat the milk until bubbles form around the edge. Using a tablespoon, drop mounds of meringue onto the milk; do not crowd the pan. Poach gently for about 4 minutes, turning once. Adjust the heat to prevent milk from boiling. Remove the meringues with a slotted spoon or skimmer. Drain on paper towels. Repeat with the remaining meringue. Strain the milk into a 2-quart saucepan and use for custard sauce.

In a medium bowl, whisk together the egg yolks, the remaining ½ cup sugar, and the salt. Slowly whisk in 1½ cups of the warm milk. Whisk the egg mixture into the saucepan and cook over medium-low heat, stirring constantly, until the mixture will coat the back of a spoon. Remove from the heat and let cool. Stir in the Amaretto.

Pour the cooled custard into a serving dish. Place the poached meringues on top and chill. To serve, sprinkle the meringues with chopped almonds.

DECEMBER

CHRISTMAS AT HOME

When it comes to Christmas celebrations, I believe the earlier, the merrier. I'm already getting ideas for December party menus when the Thanksgiving leftovers are still in the fridge!

I get into the holiday spirit as soon as the store window displays go up, even before they light the tree at Rockefeller Center. I want to get my fill of the gifting and the eating and the singing and the toasting. That way, I'm completely satisfied when the month finally comes to a close.

To anyone who complains that the holiday has been over-commercialized, I suggest that the best antidote is to make the holiday your own by creating rituals around any of the season's activities. Add your touch and make an event of it, whether it's buying and wrapping gifts, decorating the house, or planning and cooking special treats and festive meals. Instead of buying ready-made Christmas gift wrap or ornaments or cake, you could come up with

For Christmas I deck the halls—and myself—out in red.

BARBARA AND DAN'S TOP CHRISTMAS MUSIC PICKS

Nat "King" Cole, *The Christmas Song*

Ella Fitzgerald, *Christmas*

Otis Redding, *Soul Christmas*

Johnny Mathis, *The Christmas Music of Johnny Mathis*

Aaron Neville, *Aaron Neville's Soulful Christmas*

Luther Vandross, *This Is Christmas*

The Temptations, *Give Love at Christmas*

Mariah Carey, *Merry Christmas*

Vanessa Williams, *Star Bright*

Frank Sinatra, *Christmas Songs by Sinatra*

Freddie Jackson, *At Christmas*

The Whispers, *Christmas Moments*

The O'Jays, *Home for Christmas*

Kathleen Battle and Christopher Parkening, *Angels' Glory*

Ray Charles, *"The Spirit of Christmas"**

* Our wedding song on December 23, 1992.

your own. The mother of a friend of mine makes candles every year for Christmas. Think about the things you enjoy most in life, and try to find a way of incorporating them as your own holiday customs.

One of Dan's and my customs is to surround ourselves with the sounds of the holiday season—a mix of traditional Christmas songs, jazz, R&B, and pop. Each year we go through our huge collection of holiday CDs, load our top twenty-five picks into the CD player, and leave the switch flipped to "on."

The smells of Christmas are important, too. Because the sense of smell is so intricately connected with memories, the aroma of pine that fills the house when you first bring in the Christmas tree, or the scent of juniper from a few branches in a vase, can take you back to the anticipation and excitement of childhood Christmases. For me, it's the smell of Christmas cookies baking in the oven. When I was growing up, my father was the one in charge of cookies. The rest of the year, his cooking was pretty much confined to rustling up a big weekend breakfast, but at Christmas he was the pastry chef. He made many different kinds of cookies, in batches big enough to tide four kids over through the entire holiday season. Daddy would store the cookies in big tins, layered for variety, and keep them moist by tucking an apple or a slice of bread in the container. That big supply was meant just for us and our guests. In those days, nobody thought of making little packages of home-baked cookies as gifts, because everyone made their own.

Just as my mother was a traditionalist in her menus for special occasions, my dad had a traditional repertoire for his Christmas bakeoff: oatmeal cookies, sugar cookies, chocolate chip cookies, peanut butter cookies, and my absolute favorite—mincemeat cookies. I remember sitting near the oven, willing that first batch to come out.

We all seem to find our own Christmas specialty. Whether it's baking, like my father did, or playing seasonal songs, or trimming the tree, it's the thing we do year after year without ever considering it a chore. Mine is decorating our home. I put a little bit of Christmas into every nook and cranny. You can't go into the bathroom in our house without knowing it's Christmas. There are the green and red towels and soaps and, just in case you didn't get it, a few springs of holly placed around the room. I've been known to tie ribbons around the wastepaper baskets. I use plenty of garland—sometimes boxwood, sometimes pine, depending

MINCEMEAT COOKIES

This is a variation on my dad's recipe. These cookies seem to be the most popular with our houseguests. A plate of these—warm, out of the oven, with a glass of cold milk—and I'm in heaven.

YIELDS APPROXIMATELY 6 DOZEN COOKIES

3½ cups all-purpose flour

1 teaspoon salt

1 teaspoon baking soda

1 teaspoon cinnamon

½ teaspoon allspice

1 cup vegetable shortening or butter (see Note)

1¾ cup sugar

1 teaspoon vanilla extract

3 large eggs

1 cup chopped walnuts

2 cups mincemeat

1 Place a rack in center of the oven and preheat to 350 degrees.

2 Sift together the flour, salt, baking soda, cinnamon, and allspice in a medium bowl and set aside. With the mixer, beat the shortening until creamy. Add the sugar gradually and mix until light, about 2 minutes. Add the vanilla and eggs, and beat until smooth. Add the flour mixture in two parts, beating well after each addition. Scrape the sides of the bowl with a rubber spatula if necessary. Stir in the nuts and mincemeat with the mixer on low or by hand.

3 Drop the batter by heaping teaspoonfuls, 2 inches apart on a nonstick or lightly greased cookie sheet. Bake until golden brown, about 12 to 14 minutes.

NOTE: Shortening and butter both make a good cookie.

on what I feel like. Then I have to find places to display Dan's and Dana's favorite Christmas decorations. And everywhere there are flowers, but they're always different from year to year. One year, I filled the house with masses of red roses, another with an abundance of carnations. Some years I like the purity and austerity of paperwhites, others the lush, oversized blooms of amaryllis. Last year, it looked as if giant poinsettias had taken root in every corner of the house.

But the big event is the Christmas tree. I grew up in a conventional one-tree family. Then Jane Smith, a dear friend who's president of the National Council of Negro Women, told me how every year her dad had managed to install a second Christmas tree and then a third in their house, despite her mother's protests. Eventually, it became a tradition. Her story of "The Great Tree Caper" inspired me. After we completed our house in Sag Harbor, I decided to add a second tree at Christmas. Ultimately, we came to have three. That's another one of our holiday traditions.

Our classic tree, like the one I grew up with, is in the living room. It changes from year to year—sometimes I like to put only white lights on it, other years it's colored lights, or ribbons, or bows. It depends on my mood. But every year, I hang on it some of the Christmas ornaments from the batch that Dan and I gave our guests as favors when we were married on December 23, 1992. They're clear glass, with our names and Dana's in gold. Every year, we hear from one or another of our guests who'll tell us that they, too, hang our ornament on their tree each Christmas.

Our other special tree decorations include some incredible, handblown glass ornaments designed by Christopher Radko, whom I first met when he appeared on my television show. Christopher found his calling through one of those every-cloud-has-a-silver-lining accidents. His family collected rare glass ornaments, and one year tragedy struck: The tree fell over, and the ornaments were destroyed. When Christopher tried without success to find new, handmade ones to replace them, he got the idea for his now hugely successful business. Chris's decorations have adorned trees at the White House and in the Kennedy Center.

Our second tree is our "Kwanzmas" tree. During the week of Kwanzaa, beginning on December 26, we join millions of people around

A "Kwanzmas Tree" decorated with colorful African gourds and Kente cloth bows.

Dana's Christmas tree this year is decorated with gossamer bows and pink ornaments.

the world in celebrating our African cultural heritage and the unity of our family. The holiday takes its name from the Swahili, meaning "first fruits of the harvest." Since one of its main purposes is to encourage people to look back as a means of finding a way forward, most people try to incorporate handcrafted or homemade items in their Kwanzaa observance, especially if the objects have an educational element. Our tree evolves from year to year, but it's always decorated in bold Afrocentric colors, with brightly painted gourds and other natural objects. It looks perfect standing near the kinara—the ceremonial candleholder of Kwanzaa—in our family room, which also has an Afrocentric theme.

The most whimsical of all the trees is our third one, which changes from year to year. Once it was actually a group of trees—a cluster of small pines. But for a while it's been Dana's tree. My mother provided the inspiration. She used to always make my room very pretty, with a vanity skirt she had sewn and feminine window drapes. I wanted to do the same in Dana's room for Christmas, before she reached the age when everything has to be cool. I wanted to keep that fairy-tale quality alive for her as long as possible, and to give her a dreamlike memory for the future. So I put a tree in her room for Christmas and gave it a very girlish look, with gossamer bows and pink ribbons.

The important thing is to create traditions in your own home. If you can't stand the thought of buying a living tree that you'll have to throw out in a couple of weeks, you could think about having a rosemary tree instead. Since rosemary has needles, just like pine trees, it's not such a far-fetched idea; and its aroma is even more wonderful than the aroma of evergreens. One person I know gathers large, fallen branches of willow every Christmas, sprays them white, and hangs her ornaments on them. They look very elegant, and she doesn't have to contend with a carpet of fallen needles.

At least a couple of my friends have one tree for the grown-ups and one for the kids. The adults' tree might be decorated in a sophisticated color scheme—maroon and teal; or hot pink, red, and kelly green. The kids' tree looks just the way you'd expect, festooned with colored paper rings, strands of popcorn, and a glorious hodgepodge of lights, tinsel, and every kind of ornament a sturdy little pine can hold.

Whether you bring out the same box of ornaments every Christmas or make a habit of finding new ones each year, when you decorate your tree, you are personalizing your holiday. You probably have other rituals, too, that are unique to your family. In one home that we know of, each child is assigned to help with a particular dish, and as the child grows, he or she takes over full responsibility for it. Another family takes the kids to volunteer at a soup kitchen on Christmas morning, and yet another has a Christmas Eve gift tradition of exchanging new pajamas to be unwrapped and worn that very night. One friend told me her family makes a Christmas videotape before the tree comes down every year and puts it away with the decorations. Then, the following year, they replay the tape before they put the tree up and decorate it. It's a wonderful way to watch your family grow.

A CHRISTMAS EVE FONDUE

I'm glad for this Christmas Eve breather. The stores are finally closed, the presents are all wrapped, and what isn't already done just won't get done. We now have the perfect excuse to relax over a nice meal. One of the things I love about the holidays is that the house is already looking beautiful and the trees are decorated, so I can entertain friends without having to go to much trouble. And on Christmas Eve, I like to invite over a few stray people who don't have family around with whom to celebrate. We spend a cozy evening together, sitting around the coffee table and eating fondue.

I was introduced to fondue dinners when I was modeling in Italy. Since I didn't have my own apartment, I stayed in a succession of pensiones and hotels. However lovely they were, they always felt impersonal. So when the head of my agency, Beatrice, asked me to din-

After the presents are all wrapped, kick back and relax with a small group of friends and family over a fondue pot.

ner, I was delighted to accept. It made me feel so much less of an outsider to be invited to someone's home.

I remember every detail of that dinner. Though it was a casual meal, everything about it seemed exotic. I thought it was wonderful and amusing to cook your own food right at the table. And the fondue I ate that night tasted delicious. When I got back to New York, I immediately went out and bought two pots so I, too, could serve fondue.

Those first pots I bought were not the greatest, but fondue equipment has gotten much better in the past few years. The old ones were very thin, so it was hard to keep the temperature constant. This wasn't much of an issue when it came to heating oil to cook fish or meat, but it was a serious problem when you were serving cheese or chocolate fondue. Sometimes the cheese or chocolate wasn't hot enough. More often, it would be overcooked or burned. You can almost always find one of the old fondue pots on sale in flea markets. Buy one and experiment, to see if you enjoy making this dish. If so, throw away that pot and invest in a good one.

I like the idea of serving fondue to my friends on Christmas Eve because it makes for the kind of casual, communal meal that you don't have to eat at the dinner table. I prepare a classic cheese fondue, which is very rich, and a lighter seafood fondue. I even make a chocolate fondue for dessert. I put out breads to dip into the hot cheese fondue; dipping sauces for the shrimps and scallops that people spear out of the seafood fondue; and pieces of fruit and cake to plunge into the velvety chocolate. I think the experience gives my guests, many of whom had never tasted these dishes before, something to remember for quite awhile. Try it on your friends, especially when your dinner guests include children. Though they may need some help from the grown-ups, they love this meal because it has a certain quality of being able to play with your food!

A Christmas Eve
Fondue for Six

Cheese Fondue

—

Seafood Fondue

—

Chocolate Dessert Fondue

—

Mulled Wine

—

Cabernet, Mt. Veeder, Napa Valley, 1995
(or any other Cabernet)

*At our table we have Cheese Fondue, which
we serve with breads and meats; Seafood
Fondue with shrimp, scallops, and tuna;
and Chocolate Dessert Fondue, served with
strawberries, pineapple, and bananas.*

CHEESE FONDUE

This is a sinfully delicious dish that I like to serve during the winter months. Everyone gets involved in this communal affair. Use Cognac if you have it on hand, or as the Swiss traditionally do, use Kirsch. The key to a successful cheese fondue is one of the wonderfully well-made fondue pots on the market today. If you find a pot with both high and low heat settings, that is even better. (Be sure to use special long-tined, heat-proof handled forks, and allow for no more than 6 people per fondue pot.)   SERVES 6

1 large clove garlic, sliced in half

½ cup dry white wine

¾ pound shredded Gruyère cheese

¾ pound shredded natural, unpasteurized Emmenthaler cheese

½ teaspoon hot paprika (or more to taste)

⅛ teaspoon white pepper

2 tablespoons Cognac or Kirsch

Crusty French and/or Italian bread, cut into 1-inch cubes

Salami cut into 1-inch chunks

Mini meatballs

Vegetables of choice (broccoli, bell peppers, squash, etc.) cut into bite-size pieces

Rub the insides of a fondue pot with the garlic; discard the garlic. Add the wine and warm over medium heat until hot, but not boiling. Add the cheese gradually to the wine. Reduce the heat, stirring often with a wooden spoon until the cheese has melted. Add the paprika, white pepper, and cognac; continue stirring until the fondue is thick and creamy. Using heatproof long-handled forks, have your guests dip bread cubes, salami chunks, meatballs, and vegetables into the fondue.

SEAFOOD FONDUE

SERVES 6

4 cups vegetable oil (see Note)

1 pound large uncooked shrimp, cleaned and deveined, with tails removed

1 pound fresh boneless tuna, cut into 1-inch chunks

1 pound medium-size sea scallops

Vegetables for garnish

Dijon mustard with horseradish

Wasabi Mayonnaise (recipe follows)

Chili Mayonnaise (see page 172)

In a fondue pot, over medium-high heat, warm the oil. Arrange the seafood on a platter. Garnish with vegetables. Using heatproof long-handled forks, have your guests spear chunks of seafood and cook them directly in the hot oil. Be very careful of the oil, as it may splatter. Serve with sauces.

NOTE: For subtly different flavors, you may try other oils, such as peanut or coconut.

WASABI MAYONNAISE

YIELDS ABOUT 1 CUP

1 tablespoon wasabi powder

1 tablespoon water

1 cup mayonnaise

Salt and freshly ground white pepper to taste

Mix together the wasabi powder and water. Let stand a few minutes. Mix together the mayonnaise and wasabi. Season with salt and white pepper. Keep refrigerated until used.

CHOCOLATE DESSERT FONDUE

I say go all the way with your fondue dinner, it's a terrific finale. Don't be surprised if someone in the crowd requests vanilla ice cream to spoon some chocolate over. Then, I think, the addition of crumbled cake and chopped nuts might be appropriate. (Be sure to use special long-tined, heatproof forks, and allow for no more than six people per fondue pot.) **SERVES 6**

2 cups (12 ounces) semisweet chocolate chips

1 cup heavy cream

¾ cup mini-marshmallows

1 banana, sliced into ½-inch rounds

1 pineapple, peeled, cored, and cut into 1-inch chunks

1 pint strawberries, stems removed

One 14-ounce pound cake, cut into 1-inch squares

In a fondue pot, combine the chocolate chips, cream, and marshmallows. Over medium heat, stir with a wooden spoon until chocolate and marshmallows are melted and the mixture is smooth. Arrange the fruits and cake on a serving platter. Using heatproof long-handled forks, have your guests dip fruits and cake into the chocolate fondue.

MULLED WINE

SERVES 6

2 bottles Cabernet Sauvignon

Juice of 3 lemons

½ cup superfine sugar or more to taste

4 sticks cinnamon

1 tablespoon whole cloves or more to taste

1 tablespoon whole allspice berries or freshly grated nutmeg

1 orange, sliced

1 lemon, sliced

In a large saucepan, combine the wine, lemon juice, and sugar. Stir until dissolved. Add the cinnamon, cloves, allspice or nutmeg, and orange and lemon slices. Heat, but do not boil. Lower the heat and simmer 15 minutes. Strain the wine into heated mugs and serve at once.

CHRISTMAS DINNER

I had wonderful Christmases as a child, and I share with my parents the belief that Christmas is a family day. But while my childhood Christmas consisted of huge amounts of people at my grandmother's house, today our extended family is scattered.

The way Dan, Dana, and I celebrate is very focused, and usually involves just us three. We used to stay in the apartment, but now we have the Sag Harbor house to go to. It lends itself perfectly to having a large, late, leisurely breakfast, then sitting in front of the fireplace, opening presents, listening to music, and enjoying the glorious sight of Christmas reds and golds and greens wherever we look.

For dinner I'll make a small feast just for us three, starting with a dish like oyster stew—what I think of as sophisticated comfort food. Later in the evening, after we've filled ourselves up with all the traditional holiday foods—and some, like my special mincemeat sauce, not so traditional—maybe we'll have some guests over for drinks, or to share our fluffy, white coconut-pecan cake. But for the most part, it's a lazy, very personal day. That's *our* tradition.

CHRISTMAS DINNER FOR FOUR

Collard Oyster Stew

Roasted Herb-Stuffed Capon
with Warm Mincemeat Sauce

Maple Glazed Carrots

Buttermilk Mashed Potatoes

Tangy Brussels Sprouts

Triple-Layer Coconut-Pecan Cake

Sauvignon Blanc, Lyeth Estate White, Napa Valley, 1995
(or any other Sauvignon)

*At our home Christmas dinner is a small feast.
Collard Oyster Stew, Roasted Herb-Stuffed Capon
with Warm Mincemeat Sauce, Buttermilk Mashed
Potatoes, and Tangy Brussels Sprouts are perfect
sophisticated comfort foods.*

COLLARD OYSTER STEW

SERVES 4

2 large all-purpose potatoes, peeled and diced
2 tablespoons butter
1 medium onion, chopped
2 cups chopped fresh or frozen collard greens
2 teaspoons dried thyme leaves
2 large potatoes, cooked and mashed (approximately 2 cups)
4 cups reserved oyster liquid or clam juice
1 pint fresh oysters, shucked and drained
Salt and freshly ground black pepper to taste

Boil the diced potatoes until tender. Set aside. In a large saucepan over medium heat, melt the butter. Sauté the onion in the butter until tender. Add the collard greens and thyme. Cook over low heat 20 to 25 minutes. In a blender or food processor, blend the greens mixture and mashed potatoes. Transfer to a large pot and add the oyster liquid. Bring to a boil and reduce the heat. Add the oysters, diced potatoes, salt, and pepper. Simmer about 2 minutes. Serve immediately.

ROASTED HERB-STUFFED CAPON WITH WARM MINCEMEAT SAUCE

SERVES 4

One 6- to 8-pound capon or roasting chicken
Salt and freshly ground black pepper to taste
Herbed Stuffing (recipe follows)
Melted butter for basting
Warm Mincemeat Sauce (recipe follows)

Preheat the oven to 450 degrees. Rinse the capon under cold water and dry thoroughly inside. Season the capon inside and out with salt and pepper. Stuff the body as well as the neck cavity of the capon loosely with the Herbed Stuffing. Tie the legs together with kitchen string. Rub or brush butter over the skin of the capon. Place the capon breast side up on a rack inside of a roasting pan in the oven and lower the temperature to 350 degrees. Baste frequently with pan drippings and melted butter. Roast approximately 20 minutes per pound or until the skin is golden brown and the juices of the roast run clear when it is pierced at the thigh. Let the capon rest at least 20 minutes before carving. Serve with the Warm Mincemeat Sauce.

HERBED STUFFING

There are many wonderful stuffing and dressing recipes. This one just might become a tradition in your home. The stuffing could be baked inside the cavity of your poultry or in a casserole. If you decide to stuff your capon, remove the dressing from the cavity after your meal. Refrigerate separately and reheat before serving.   SERVES 4

3 tablespoons butter

1 cup chopped onions

1 cup chopped celery

4 cups dry or slightly toasted white bread cubes

2 teaspoons poultry seasoning

2 teaspoons chopped fresh sage leaves or ¾ teaspoon dried sage leaves

2 teaspoons finely chopped fresh thyme leaves or ¾ teaspoon dried thyme leaves

2 teaspoons finely chopped fresh parsley

2 large eggs, lightly beaten

½ to 1 cup chicken stock

Salt and freshly ground black pepper to taste

In a sauté pan, melt the butter. Sauté the onions and celery in the butter until tender. In a large bowl, toss the bread cubes with the onions, celery, poultry seasoning, and herbs. Add the eggs and enough chicken stock to slightly moisten and barely bind ingredients. Season with salt and pepper to taste.

WARM MINCEMEAT SAUCE

I love this sauce. You might want to try it with poultry or wild fowl, and the orange zest is a nice addition.   YIELDS 3 CUPS

2 cups roasting-pan drippings and/or chicken stock

1 cup bottled mincemeat

¼ cup port

1 tablespoon cornstarch

1 tablespoon cold water

1 tablespoon grated orange zest (optional)

In a small saucepan, heat the drippings and/or chicken stock. Add the mincemeat and port and stir in until blended. Simmer 5 to 8 minutes. In a small cup, mix together the cornstarch and cold water until dissolved. Stir into the sauce. Let simmer about 2 to 3 more minutes, until desired thickness. Add zest, and serve warm.

MAPLE-GLAZED CARROTS

SERVES 4

6 medium carrots, peeled and cut
into 1-inch rounds
2 tablespoons butter
1 teaspoon ground ginger
1 teaspoon ground nutmeg
½ cup maple syrup

Place the carrots in a medium saucepan, add water to cover. Bring to a boil, and cook the carrots until tender, about 15 minutes. Drain. Add the butter, ginger, nutmeg, and maple syrup. Stir to coat. Simmer the carrots until well glazed. Serve immediately.

BUTTERMILK MASHED POTATOES

SERVES 4

2 pounds Red Bliss potatoes, unpeeled
⅔ cup buttermilk
¼ cup (½ stick) butter
Salt and freshly ground black pepper to taste

Scrub the potatoes. Cut in half, and place in a medium saucepan. Cover with cold water and bring to a boil. Cook until the potatoes are tender, about 20 minutes. Drain; add the buttermilk and butter. Mash until creamy. Season with salt and pepper. Serve immediately.

TANGY BRUSSELS SPROUTS

SERVES 4

1 pound Brussels sprouts
1 cup chicken stock
2 tablespoons butter
1 teaspoon dry mustard
1 teaspoon salt
1 teaspoon ground white pepper

Remove any wilted outer leaves from the Brussels sprouts. Cut off the stems. Soak the sprouts in cold water. Drain well. In a medium saucepan, place chicken stock and the Brussels sprouts. Cook, covered, until barely tender, about 10 minutes. Drain. Add the butter, dry mustard, salt, and white pepper. Toss the Brussels sprouts to coat. Sauté for 2 minutes. Serve immediately.

TRIPLE-LAYER COCONUT-PECAN CAKE

SERVES 12

CAKE

3 cups cake flour

1 tablespoon baking powder

¼ teaspoon salt

1 cup (2 sticks) butter, softened

2 cups sugar

4 large eggs, at room temperature

2 large egg yolks

2 teaspoons vanilla extract

1¼ cups unsweetened coconut milk

FILLING

1 large egg

⅓ cup granulated sugar

⅓ cup brown sugar

5 ounces evaporated milk

6 tablespoons butter

¼ cup coconut-flavored rum

2 cups sweetened shredded coconut

1½ cup toasted, chopped pecans

FROSTING

1¼ cups light corn syrup

2 large egg whites

¼ teaspoon coconut extract

2 cups sweetened shredded coconut, divided

To make the cake, preheat the oven to 350 degrees. Grease three 9-inch round cake pans and line the bottoms with waxed paper. Grease the paper and dust the pans with flour, tapping out the excess. Into a medium bowl, sift the flour, baking powder, and salt. In a large bowl, with the electric mixer on medium speed, beat the butter until creamy. Gradually beat in the sugar. Beat 2 minutes, until light and fluffy. Beat in the whole eggs one at a time until well blended. Beat in the yolks and vanilla. With the mixer on low speed, alternately beat in the flour mixture and the coconut milk, beginning and ending with the flour mixture, beating until blended. Divide the batter among the pans, spreading evenly.

Bake 25 to 30 minutes, until a toothpick inserted in the center of the cakes comes out clean. Cool the cakes in the pans 10 minutes. Run a knife around the sides and turn out onto wire racks to cool.

To make the filling, in a medium saucepan, with a fork, beat the egg. Add the sugars, evaporated milk, and butter. Cook over medium heat, stirring constantly, until the filling boils. Remove from heat and stir in the rum, coconut, and pecans. Transfer to a small bowl and let cool.

To make the frosting, in a small saucepan, bring the corn syrup to a boil. In a large bowl, with the electric mixer on medium speed, beat the egg whites until soft peaks form. With the mixer on high speed, gradually drizzle hot corn syrup in a thin, steady stream. Beat until stiff peaks form. Beat in the coconut extract. Fold in 1 cup of the coconut.

To assemble, place one cake layer on a serving plate. Spread with half of the filling. Top with another cake layer and spread with the remaining filling. Top with the last cake layer. Spread the sides and top of the cake with frosting. Sprinkle with the remaining 1 cup of coconut, pressing to stick to the frosting.

A New Year's Eve Pajama Party for Kids

New Year's Eve is the night of all nights—the time to put the past behind you, the moment when the bright new year holds nothing but promise. To hold tight to this feeling of infinite possibility, we want to spend the evening mingling with the most interesting people in the most exciting place and having the most possible fun.

I have spent many a happy New Year's Eve enjoying the city's glamour in the comfort of my New York restaurant. We have a very elegant, black-tie event. Anyone who wants to feel part of the excitement of Times Square, which is practically the center of the world on New Year's Eve, can watch

New Year's Eve is a two-stop party: an early slumber party for kids, complete with Chicken Tenders and Cheddar Cheese Soup, and later on, a midnight Champagne toast for the adults!

the throngs in the street through our picture windows or from the vantage point of our rooftop café. Outside, there's the bustle of thousands of merry-makers; and inside, everything is warm and lovely.

But if I weren't at B. Smith's, I'd celebrate New Year's Eve as my parents did—at home. On the biggest party night of the year, they joined my brothers and me in front of the television set, and along with nearly two billion others, we watched the New Year's Eve show put on by Guy Lombardo and his Royal Canadians. The images of the glamorous partygoers at the Waldorf, dressed to the nines and whirling around the room, and the bustle of the raucous crowds jostling in the cold on Broadway, kept us spellbound and wide awake until the Times Square countdown vaulted us into another New Year.

It was exciting to watch the crowds gathered in New York City, but I certainly didn't want to be there. I considered myself in the best of all places to welcome the New Year—nestled in the comfort and security of our living room and snuggled up on the sofa, with the people I loved reassuringly close. I never imagined that one day I'd be part of the New York world I was watching on TV, any more than several years later, I'd imagine that my picture of a perfect New Year's Eve would end up being very close to the one of my childhood. If I had my way, I'd spend it in my own home and in the company of my family and closest friends.

We'd have a two-stop party—an early celebration just for kids, and a later one for the rest of us. I'd serve the children a dinner of Cheddar cheese soup and chicken tenders—which are just sophisticated enough for parents to munch on, too. Then I'd set the kids up with their sleeping bags, since they love any excuse for a slumber party. Once they'd gone to sleep—or at least once they'd settled down—the rest of us would do our own thing: listen to music, play cards, or just chat and enjoy one another's company.

I'd put out some platters of special-occasion treats—caviar and smoked salmon, pâté and triple crème fraîche, plus petits fours and Champagne. Naturally, I'd get out the noisemakers and the silly hats, a few balloons, and bags of confetti. And at the stroke of midnight, we'd wish one another a happy New Year, one filled with many rituals and celebrations.

A New Year's Eve Pajama Party for Kids

Cheddar Cheese Soup

Sweet-and-Sour Chicken Tenders

Chocolate Cookie
Ice Cream Sandwiches

Sparkling cider

CHEDDAR CHEESE SOUP

If this savory dish is a little too rich and thick for your family's taste, just thin it with a little chicken stock.   SERVES 4

4 tablespoons (½ stick) unsalted butter
½ cup finely chopped onion
1½ cups finely chopped celery
2 tablespoons all-purpose flour
4 cups rich chicken stock
1½ cups milk
2 cups grated Cheddar cheese

In a large saucepan over medium heat, melt the butter. Sauté the onion and celery until softened. Stir in the flour, and you have a roux that should be cooked for 3 minutes, stirring frequently. Gradually add the stock, whisking until smooth. Bring to a boil, add the milk, reduce the heat, and simmer until thickened. Stir in the cheese gradually until it is melted. Do not boil. Serve hot with croutons on top or crackers on the side.

SWEET-AND-SOUR CHICKEN TENDERS

SERVES 4

¼ cup all-purpose flour
1 teaspoon Creole seasoning
½ teaspoon freshly ground black pepper
½ cup vegetable oil
2 pounds boneless skinless chicken breast, cut into ½-inch strips
Sweet-and-Sour Sauce (recipe follows)

Mix the flour and seasonings together. In a medium skillet, heat the oil. Dredge the chicken in the seasoned flour. Place the chicken in the skillet. Do not overcrowd the chicken. Cook in batches, if necessary, turning with tongs until the tenders are golden brown. Remove and drain on paper towels. Toss with Sweet-and-Sour Sauce. Serve immediately.

SWEET-AND-SOUR SAUCE

YIELDS 1 CUP

½ cup ketchup
1 teaspoon soy sauce
1 teaspoon cider vinegar
½ cup brown sugar
1 tablespoon cornstarch
½ cup orange juice

In a small saucepan, combine the ketchup, soy sauce, vinegar, and brown sugar. Over medium-high heat, bring the sauce to a boil, stirring occasionally. Reduce the heat. In a small cup, mix the cornstarch into the orange juice until dissolved. Stir into the sauce and simmer, stirring occasionally, until the sauce thickens, approximately 5 minutes.

CHOCOLATE COOKIE ICE CREAM SANDWICHES

Ice cream sandwiches bring out the kid in everyone. You might want to put out a few plates filled with different colored sprinkles, so kids of all ages can turn their sandwiches on their sides and roll them in the sprinkles for an extra treat.

YIELDS 14 SANDWICHES

2 cups all-purpose flour
1 cup unsweetened cocoa powder
1 teaspoon baking powder
½ teaspoon salt
¼ teaspoon baking soda
1 cup unsalted butter, at room temperature
1 cup packed brown sugar
1 cup granulated sugar
3 large eggs
2½ teaspoons vanilla extract
4½ pints ice cream

Preheat the oven to 350 degrees. Lightly grease several large cookie sheets. Sift the flour, cocoa, baking powder, salt, and baking soda into a medium bowl. In a large bowl, with electric mixer on medium speed, beat the butter until creamy. Gradually beat in the sugars, and beat until light, about 5 minutes. Beat in the eggs and vanilla until combined. Beat in half the flour mixture, then stir in the remaining flour mixture until well blended. Drop the dough by heaping tablespoons onto the prepared cookie sheets, 3 inches apart. Bake 12 to 14 minutes, until the cookies spring back when lightly pressed in the center. Let cool on the sheet 1 minute, then remove to a wire rack to cool. The cookies can be stored in an airtight container until needed. Just before serving, let the ice cream soften in the refrigerator 30 minutes before assembling the sandwiches.

ACKNOWLEDGMENTS

To my husband, Dan Gasby, thanks for really knowing how to pick 'em and finding me a great literary agent in, of all places, Minneapolis. Jonathan Lazear worked his special style of magic, securing for me a home at Random House. To Ann Godoff, Random House president and publisher, a woman with vision—thank you for believing in *my* vision. To Pamela Cannon, who deftly wore two hats, serving both as super-editor and as strategic-thinking publicist on the book. A big thank-you goes out to the wonderful team at Random House who helped put this book together, including Beth Pearson, Stacy Rockwood, Kathy Rosenbloom, and Robin Schiff.

A heartfelt note of thanks to my wonderful co-writer Barbara Aria, who helped bring my thoughts, ideas, and stories to the page, and to Joel Avirom, whose inspired sense of design helped to make this book come alive.

After I finished my first book, I decided that the most important mandate I would give myself when starting this second project was to make sure to have fun throughout the entire process. With that thought in mind, I went about gathering a talented group of people who understood my creative vision and playful style.

As luck would have it, right before I made a final decision on a photographer for this book, I met photographer Mark Ferri. Immediately his style and eye, as well as—just as important—his overall demeanor, were perfectly in tune with mine. Mark, thank you for allowing me to look through your lens and make suggestions. And you were more than ably assisted by Marcus Accord in New York and Susan Lindsay Wagner in Orlando.

Many thanks to makeup artist and friend Daniel Green, who was always open to lending a helping hand, and always made me look absolutely beautiful; hair designer Darryl Bennet, who worked wonders with my hair, and who always had a righteous attitude and a beautiful smile. Zianni Coats did a terrific makeup job during our Washington, D.C., shoot.

Now, when you have great hair and makeup professionals at the ready, you need someone who can pull your look together just the way you want it. I am indeed fortunate to have had the woman I fondly call "style mama," fashion stylist extraordinaire Ionia Dunn-Lee.

A lifestyle book would not be complete without food stylists and recipe developers: Jeanne Voltz, Rhonda Stieglitz, Joanne Rubin, Cyn Raftus MacDowell, Chris Kougy, Sarah Reynolds, Jill Raff, Allie Brodhead, Justin Poldino, and Karen Donahue.

The major job of prop styling was handled with unique flair—and a grand sense of humor—by Frank Way and Cyn Raftus MacDowell. Thanks also to Frank's parents, Fi and D. Way, and to Darrell Smith, Walt Disney World VIP tour guide par excellence, in Orlando, Florida.

Craft designer-artists Mary Emery, Amy Manchester Hawkes, and Genevieve Sterbenz translated my creative visions into realities, for which I am grateful.

This book would not have been as much fun to produce without the guests who gave their time and company at the dinners, parties, and special events that we photographed. Thanks to Tom Townsend; Nathaniel and Lois Young; Kenneth Ward; James and Tia Oakley and their two sons, Jay and Jordan Oakley; Tanya Touchstone; Carolyn and Troy Weaver; Walter and Jean Somerville; Julian Tait; Kia Jones; Malik and TJ Ali for their little girls, Dylan and Shara Ali; Kari Edgecom; Tamika Bush; Ron Donovan; Mic Murphy; Edward Robinson; Clarice Taylor; Cynthia Badie; Christine Buechtling; Rich Moran; Helene Jenkins; Joanne and Bob Carter; Henry and Patricia Chung and their daughter, Felicia; Lily Yu; Jack Christou; and the kids in pajamas, Teddy, Kanjan, Alexander, and Aluna.

Anneli McDowell, Janice De Rosa, Marcia Edlich, Ted Conklin and Tara Newman, and Harry P. Leu Gardens graciously allowed us to use their homes and gardens for location photography.

Finally, I want to thank Grayce Galiato, my personal executive assistant, who helps me keep my world together; and Ed Arronson, for lending us his help and his lovely wife, Adrienne Hammel, who did a fabulous job as production coordinator, on call at all hours. I couldn't have completed this project without her.

ACKNOWLEDGMENTS

CREDITS

JANUARY

A NEW YEAR'S DAY BUFFET

China: Lenox China

Votives: Broadway Panhandler

Candlesticks: Crate & Barrel

Dress (page 2): courtesy of A.B.S.

Sweater and skirt (center, page 7): courtesy of Carmen Marc Valvo

A CHINESE NEW YEAR DINNER

Tablecloth: TableToppers

Green plates, blue pottery bowls, green soup tureen: Felissimo

Votives, cutlery: Adhoc Softwares

FEBRUARY

A VALENTINE'S DAY DINNER FOR TWO

Tablecloth: TableToppers

Stemware, plates, votives: Fishs Eddy

Flatware: April Cornell

Memory box mementos: B. Smith's personal collection

B.'s suit (page 26): courtesy of Cynthia Rowley

A MARDI GRAS BUFFET

Serving containers: Crate & Barrel

Plates: Broadway Panhandler

Ornaments: Christopher Radko

MARCH

DANA'S RITE-OF-PASSAGE DINNER

Carved animal figures, mud cloth tablecloth, napkin rings: Bamboula

Black pottery, plant pot: Museum for African Art

Shell dinner plates: Adhoc Softwares

Napkins: Crate & Barrel

Wooden bowl: Maison Provence

APRIL

AN EASTER DINNER

Stemware, napkin rings, dinner plates: Crate & Barrel

Water glasses, green chargers, oval platter, serving bowl: Fishs Eddy

Napkins: April Cornell

Garden Easter basket—wooden Easter eggs, garden stakes, plant tags, tools: Lillian Vernon catalog

Suggested reading: To Dye For: Twenty-five Great Dyeing Ideas for the Home by Juliet Bawden (Overlook Press, $15.95)

For more home decorating ideas using dyes, write to Rit, P.O. Box 307 Dept. PR 98-1, Coventry, CT 06238.

A SPRING HOOKY DAY LUNCHEON

Black pottery: Museum for African Art

Wine goblet, napkins: Pier One Imports

Flatware: B. Smith's personal collection

MAY

A MOTHER'S DAY CELEBRATION FOR MOTHERS AND OTHERS

Plates, stemware, napkins, napkin rings: Villeroy & Boch

Silverware: Antique Lenox

Flowers: Bloom

B.'s dress (page 82): courtesy of Pamela Dennis

Guest's dress (page 82): courtesy of Daphne's

A MEMORIAL DAY BARBECUE

Flatware: Crate & Barrel

Basket: Crate & Barrel

Napkins: Adhoc Softwares

Pet lover's gift basket—dog diary, Le Pooch dog perfume, Lady Barkiva dog biscuits, Watch Dog collar, Puppy Tales scrapbook, and photo album: Not Just Dogs; *wooden frame, dog bowls:* IKEA catalog (items have been modified)

JUNE

A JUNETEENTH CELEBRATION

Kente cloth: Museum for African Art

JULY

A JULY FOURTH CRAB BOIL

Table: Pine Appeal

A SUMMER SANDWICH PICNIC

Basket: Broadway Panhandler

AUGUST

A FAMILY REUNION

*For help in planning your reunion, contact
Reunions Magazine,* P.O. Box 11727,
Milwaukee, WI 53211. *They'll send you
a very helpful workbook for $10.*

B.'s suit (pages 134, 139):
courtesy of Lafayette 148

B.'s suit (page 144):
courtesy of George Simonton

SEPTEMBER

A LABOR DAY WEEKEND DINNER PARTY

Napkins, hurricane lamps, glasses: Crate & Barrel
Other items: B. Smith's personal collection

A BID WHIST CARD PARTY

Glassware: Crate & Barrel

Tablecloths: TableToppers

Suggested reading: How to Play Bid Whist by
Angel C. Beck (Zwita Productions, $6.95 plus
$2.50 postage and handling), P.O. Box 112486,
Stamford, CT 06911

For bid whist rules and other information:
http://www.bidwhist.com

OCTOBER

AN AT-HOME WINE TASTING WITH HORS D'OEUVRES

*Goblets, aluminum-and-leather tray,
leather wine rack:* Felissimo

Square tray: Crate & Barrel

HALLOWEEN DINNER IN A CAULDRON

Soup bowls, napkins: Broadway Panhandler

Ornaments on small tree: Christopher Radko

Gourd craft project supplies and materials:
the Caning Shop catalog

Japanese-style saw: Takagi Tools.

*Suggested reading: The Complete Book
of Gourd Craft* by Ginger Summit and
Jim Widess (Lark Books, $18.95)

Black shirt (page 177):
courtesy of Hino & Malee

Vest (page 177): courtesy of
Michael Simon Designs

NOVEMBER

THANKSGIVING DINNER

China and flatware: Lenox China

*Cranberry sauce glass bowl, platter, small glass stem
bowl, dessert plate:* Crate & Barrel

Green casserole, potato casserole: Fishs Eddy

Black pottery: Museum for African Art

Tablecloth: TableToppers

Suit (page 184):
courtesy of Carmen Marc Valvo

Jewelry (page 184):
courtesy of Bernie of New York

A DESSERT-DANCE PARTY

*Trifle bowl, round and shallow bowls, sauce goblet,
silver charger:* Crate & Barrel

Flowers: Bloom

DECEMBER

CHRISTMAS AT HOME

B.'s dress (page 204):
courtesy of Pam McMahon

A CHRISTMAS EVE FONDUE

Fondue pots: Le Creuset

Votives: Broadway Panhandler

Stemware, napkins, napkin rings, silver charger:
Crate & Barrel

Plates, red bowl: Fishs Eddy

Knit suit (page 212): courtesy of Rena Lange

CHRISTMAS DINNER

China, flatware: Lenox China

Napkins, ornaments, stemware:
Crate & Barrel

Assorted candlesticks: Villeroy & Boch

A NEW YEAR'S EVE PAJAMA PARTY FOR KIDS

Pillow Buddies sleeping bags:
the Company Store catalog

Dishes, platters: Fishs Eddy

B.'s suit (pages 227, 229): courtesy of Joan Vass

RESOURCES

Adhoc Softwares
410 West Broadway
New York, NY 10012
212-925-2652

April Cornell
487 Columbus Avenue
New York, NY 10024
212-799-4342

Bamboula Ltd. (trade only)
147 West 25th Street
New York, NY 10001
212-675-2714

Bloom
16 West 21st Street
New York, NY 10010
212-620-5666

Broadway Panhandler
477 Broome Street
New York, NY 10013
212-966-3434

The Caning Shop
800-544-3373
http://www.caning.com

Christopher Radko
http://www.christopherradko.com

The Company Store
800-285-3696

Crate & Barrel
650 Madison Avenue
New York, NY 10022
212-308-0011

Fishs Eddy
889 Broadway
New York, NY 10003
212-420-9020

High Tide Harry's
925 North Semoran Boulevard
Orlando, FL 32807
407-273-4422

Felissimo
10 West 56th Street
New York, NY 10019
212-247-5656

IKEA
800-434-IKEA
http://www.ikea.com

Le Creuset of America, Inc.
800-877-CREUSET

Lenox China (includes Gorham flatware)
800-63LENOX
http://www.lenox.com

Lillian Vernon
800-505-2250

Maison Provence
142 Wooster Street
New York, NY 10012
212-420-0535

Museum for African Art
593 Broadway
New York, NY 10012
212-966-1313

Pine Appeal
119 East Morse Boulevard
Winter Park, FL 32807
407-647-1868

Table Toppers
7 Shade Lane
Stamford, CT 06903
203-329-9977

Takagi Tools
800-891-7855

Villeroy & Boch
974 Madison Avenue
New York, NY 10021
212-535-2500

RECIPE INDEX

BARBARA SMITH is the host of her own half-hour nationally syndicated television series, *B. Smith with Style,* and appears regularly as a lifestyle expert on NBC's *Today* show. She is the owner of three B. Smith's restaurants, in New York City, Washington, D.C., and Sag Harbor, Long Island. Her new magazine, *B. Smith Style,* will be available on newsstands in fall 1999. She lives with her husband, Dan Gasby, a television producer, and her stepdaughter, Dana, in New York City and Sag Harbor.